Kiltubrid, County Leitrim

Maynooth Studies in Local History

SERIES EDITOR Raymond Gillespie

This is one of six short books published in the Maynooth Studies in Local History series in 2005. Like their predecessors they are, in the main, drawn from theses presented for the MA course in local history at NUI Maynooth. Also, like their predecessors, they range widely over the local experience in the Irish past. That local experience is presented in the context of the complex social and political world of which it is part, from the great houses of Armagh to the rural housing of Leitrim and from the property developers of eighteenth-century Dublin to those who rioted on the streets of the capital. The local experience cannot be a simple chronicling of events relating to an area within administrative or geographically-determined boundaries since understanding the local world presents much more complex challenges for the historian. It is an investigation of the socially diverse worlds of poor and rich. It explores the lives of those who joined the British army in the First World War as well as those who, on principle, chose not to do so. Reconstructing such diverse local worlds relies on understanding what the people of the different communities that made up the localities of Ireland had in common and what drove them apart. Understanding the assumptions, often unspoken, around which these local societies operated is the key to recreating the world of the Irish past and gaining insight into how the people who inhabited those worlds lived their daily lives. As such, studies such as those presented in these short books, together with their predecessors, are at the forefront of Irish historical research and represent some of the most innovative and exciting work being undertaken in Irish history today. They also provide models that others can follow and adapt in their own studies of the Irish past. In such ways can we better understand the regional diversity of Ireland and the social and cultural basis of that diversity. If these books also convey something of the vibrancy and excitement of the world of Irish local history today they will have achieved at least some of their purpose.

Maynooth Studies in Local History: Number 60

Kiltubrid, County Leitrim
Snapshots of a rural parish in the 1890s

Liam Kelly

FOUR COURTS PRESS

Set in 10pt on 12pt Bembo by
Carrigboy Typesetting Services, County Cork for
FOUR COURTS PRESS LTD
7 Malpas Street, Dublin 8, Ireland
e-mail: info@four-courts-press.ie
http://www.four-courts-press.ie
and in North America for
FOUR COURTS PRESS
c/o ISBS, 920 N.E. 58th Avenue, Suite 300, Portland, OR 97213.

© Liam Kelly 2005

ISBN 1–85182–898–2

All rights reserved. Without limiting the rights under copyright reserved alone, no part of this publication may be reproduced, stored in or introduced into a retrieval system, or transmitted, in any form or by any means (electronic, mechanical, photocopying, recording or otherwise), without the prior written permission of both the copyright owner and the above publisher of this book.

Printed in Ireland by
Betaprint Ltd, Dublin

Contents

Acknowledgments 6
Introduction 7
1 Houses 10
2 Land 25
3 People 38
Conclusion 59
Notes 61

FIGURES

1.1 Map of Co. Leitrim showing Kiltubrid parish 8
2.1 Pat McManus' cottage in the townland of Aughrim 11
2.2 Map of Kiltubrid showing changes in number of houses 15
2.3 Total number of houses in Kiltubrid at ten-year intervals 17
2.4 The percentage of houses in each class in Co. Leitrim 17
2.5 The percentage of houses in Kiltubrid with the different number of rooms in 1901 18
2.6 An Irish cottage of the worst kind 20
2.7 Map of Kiltubrid showing the distribution of the poorest houses in 1901 22
2.8 Laheen House 23
2.9 Driney House 24
3.1 Meitheal building hay-rick 27
3.2 Some farm tools used in Kiltubrid in the 1890s 28
3.3 The percentage of holdings in Kiltubrid in 1901 with the various type of farm buildings 34
3.4 The percentage of holdings in Kiltubrid in the various size categories in 1856 37
4.1 The population of Kiltubrid 39
4.2 The number who emigrated from Co. Leitrim at ten-year intervals from 1852 to 1892 40
4.3 Map of Kiltubrid showing marriage patterns in the 1890s 43
4.4 Photograph of McManus family 47
4.5 Photograph of Slacke family at Annadale House 49
4.6 Photograph of Mrs Mary Ward 50
4.7 Photograph of Mikey Lynch 51

TABLES

3.1 Average quantity of land in statute acres used for the various purposes in 1894 on holdings of about £4 valuation 31
3.2 Receipts and expenditure of a typical family of six persons living in Kiltubrid in 1894 on a holding of about £4 valuation 32
3.3 Corn crops in Leitrim by hundred-weight for the year 1892 36
3.4 Green crops by ton weight produced in Leitrim in 1892 36
4.1 Counties with the highest rate of seasonal migration in Ireland in the year 1891 40

Acknowledgments

My thanks to Prof. Raymond Gillespie and the Department of Modern History NUI Maynooth, for facilitating this work. I wish to thank Prof. Vincent Comerford for his help, encouragement and gentle guidance. My thanks to Dr Terence Dooley who was ever willing to help and Dr Jacinta Prunty for her advice on map-making.

The staff in the National Archives of Ireland, the National Library of Ireland, Maynooth College Library and Leitrim County Library were always courteous and helpful. I thank Elizabeth Mans for permitting me to use the photographs of Leland L. Duncan. My thanks also to Fr Seamus McKeown, parish priest of Kiltubrid, who gave me access to the parish records.

Thanks to Fionnuala Ní Mhórdha for her proof-reading and to Mary McCabe who came to the rescue whenever the computer refused to respond to my muddled instructions.

Finally thanks to my family, friends and the parishioners of Denn who had to put up with my distracted ways while this work was being done.

Introduction

The subject of this study is the rural parish of Kiltubrid, Co. Leitrim, in the 1890s. Kiltubrid, a parish of 12,088 acres and 82 townlands, is situated in south Leitrim, almost equidistant from the towns of Carrick-on-Shannon, Drumshanbo, Ballinamore and Mohill (fig. 1.1). The ecclesiastical and civil parishes of Kiltubrid are similar. Approximately one quarter of the parish is made up of lakes, woodland and bog. The parish stretches, at its northern end, to the top of Slieve an Iarainn mountain, a height of 1,927 feet and the highest point in Co. Leitrim. In this study I propose to look at this parish in the 1890s from three different perspectives: the dwelling houses, the agricultural economy and the people who lived there.

The first chapter examines the built environment of Kiltubrid in late Victorian times. In particular it will look at the dwelling houses of the people and how these had evolved since the beginning of the 19th century. The impact of the Famine on the number and style of houses will be noted and how this varied from townland to townland within the parish. By the end of the 19th century a total of 78 per cent of the houses in Kiltubrid were of the traditional Irish cottage type. These houses were second class, three-roomed and with stone walls and thatched roofs. Yet despite this apparent uniformity there was great variation in the size of the houses and the quality of materials used in them.

The second chapter deals with the agricultural economy of the period and traces the development or lack of it in farming practices since the beginning of the 19th century. The boom in the agricultural economy, which affected much of Ireland in the decades immediately after the Famine, left Leitrim largely untouched. In the 1890s the farming methods in Kiltubrid were still rather primitive and the agricultural economy depressed. Horses, which were relatively common in much of Ireland, were scarce in Kiltubrid. Farms were small, asses were plentiful and much of the farm work had to be done by manual labour. The farm buildings give an insight into the agricultural economy of the time and emphasize the centrality of cattle and pigs to that economy. Kiltubrid was a place people lived rather than made their living at this time. Households survived because one or more members of the family were earning money elsewhere, either as emigrants or seasonal migrants, and sending it back home.

The third chapter focuses on the people who lived in the parish in the 1890s. The seasonal migration that began before the Famine and the

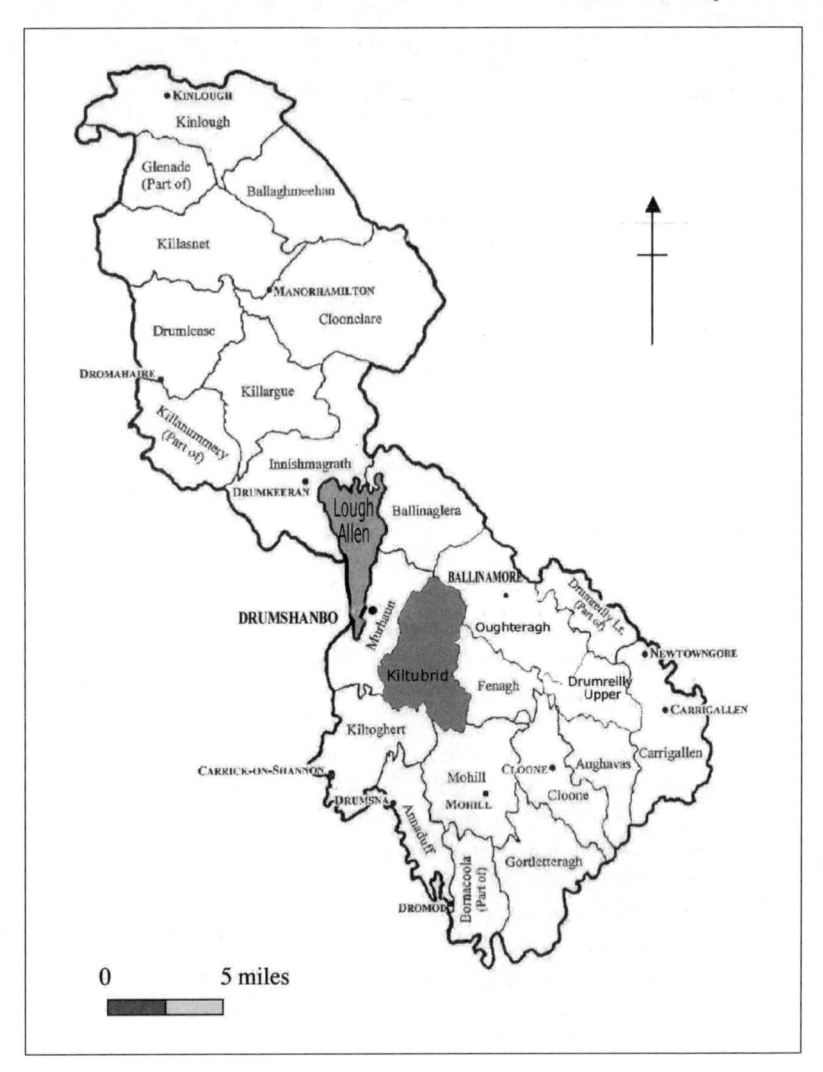

1.1 Map of Co. Leitrim showing Kiltubrid parish

emigration triggered off by it are looked at and the dramatic reduction in the overall population is traced. In this chapter there will be an attempt to identify the communities that existed within the parish in the 1890s mainly through studying the marriage patterns of the time and the Gaelic Athletic Association clubs that were set up in the parish between the years 1889 and 1892. This chapter will also take a close-up look at certain families and individuals in order to try to understand the people of this period, their way of life, the way they dress and the food they eat.

Introduction

Perhaps the most important primary source for the study of Kiltubrid parish in this period is the collection of approximately 150 photographs taken by Leland L. Duncan between 1889 and 1894. Duncan (1862–1923) lived in London and worked in the War Office there. Many of his summer holidays in the 1880s and 1890s were spent in Kiltubrid where he visited his cousins, the Slackes of Annadale. While there he attempted to record with his camera the people he met, their houses, their farm tools and their way of life. These photographs are owned by Elizabeth Mans, a descendant of the Slacke family, who lives in west Cork.[1] Many of Duncan's photographs have been published in Liam Kelly, *The face of time* (Dublin, 1995). These photographs will be used throughout this study as a primary source and it is hoped that this will strengthen the argument for using photographs as a primary source in the study of local history.

This short book will look at the lives of ordinary people in a rural parish in the north west of Ireland in the somewhat neglected decade of the 1890s. Kiltubrid was designated a 'congested district' under the terms of the 1891 Land Act. It was designated a congested district, not so much because of the density of its population but rather because of the poverty of its people. I have used the word 'snapshots' in the title of this study in both the broader sense and the narrower photographic sense of that word. It is hoped that the snapshots, both pictorial and written, contained in this work will give an insight into lives of the people of Kiltubrid in the last decade of the 19th century.

1. Houses

The built environment of a particular place and time can provide much insight into the lives of the people who lived there. A considerable amount of building went on in the parish of Kiltubrid in the last two decades of the 19th century. The new parochial house was built in 1878. St Brigid's Church at Drumcong was virtually rebuilt and transformed from being a small barn church into a large cruciform one in 1891.[1] The church bell bears the inscription 'erected by the parishioners of Kiltubrid, 1892, the Revd Hugh Brennan'.[2] Most of the National Schools in the parish were built in the 1890s.[3] This splurge of building would suggest, not just that the parish priests, Patrick O'Farrell (1876–80) and Hugh Brennan (1880–96), had energy and drive, but also that the people of the parish had a new sense of confidence and optimism as the century was coming to an end. The Cavan and Leitrim narrow gauge railway, which bisected the parish, began operations in 1887 and was another sign of hope for the area.[4] However, it is the dwelling houses of the ordinary people that tell us most about the people who lived in them.

When Leland L. Duncan photographed the house of Pat McManus in the townland of Aughrim, parish of Kiltubrid, Co. Leitrim in the month of August 1894, he was doing so to show his friends back in London, where he worked at the War Office, what the houses looked like in the rural north west of Ireland at this time[5] (fig. 2.1). In Leitrim and much of the north west of Ireland the vernacular houses at this time were mostly direct-entry, stone walled, three-roomed gabled houses with pinned thatch for roofing.[6] In the year 1901 a total of 78 per cent of the houses in Kiltubrid were of this type.[7]

Duncan's photograph, with its carefully chosen angle, is an important primary source for the study of this place in this period. We can discover details about the McManus house from this photograph which are not available in other sources. We learn that it was a gabled house with pinned thatching and that it had small-pane sash windows,[8] that it was a central hearth house and that the front wall was whitewashed. This photograph, like most Victorian photographs, is a posed one. The positioning of young Michael McManus beside the doorway and the farm tools, turf barrow and large pot nearer the camera, was deliberate. But this does not take from the value of the picture. A house, unlike a human being, cannot easily be dressed up for a photograph. This photograph, when taken along with the photograph of the hearth inside,[9] provides us with a better and more graphic depiction of the house than any written sources could possibly give.

Houses

2.1 Pat McManus' cottage in the townland of Aughrim, August 1894

Yet these photographs, despite their usefulness as primary sources, have their weaknesses. They do not provide us with any precise measurements of the house. We need to check another source, the 1901 Census, to confirm that it is a three-roomed house. We cannot generalise from the particular and conclude that all three-roomed houses in the area were exactly like this one.[10] This photograph is just a snapshot, admittedly a very good and useful one, of a particular house on a particular date. It is true that the house may not have been much different the week before or even the year after this photograph was taken. However, human habitations are always evolving. Despite the fact that more than three-quarters of the houses in Kiltubrid were very similar to the McManus house at this time there was, nevertheless, a great variety of dwelling houses in the parish in the 1890s. The number and type of houses in Kiltubrid at the end of the century was very different to those found there at beginning of the 1800s. We need written sources to trace this development.

In Leitrim and much of the west of Ireland one-roomed dwelling houses were almost as common at the beginning of the 19th century as the three-roomed houses were at the end of it. James McParlan, writing about Leitrim in 1802, said that the one-roomed houses in the county were similar to Gillo's house described in this verse:

> At one of th' ends he kept his cows,
> At th' other end he kept his spouse ...
> Without partition, or a skreen,
> Or spreading curtain, drawn between ...[11]

These houses varied in length from 12 to 18 feet long and were approximately 11 feet wide.[12] Arthur Young gave a detailed description of them:

> Mud walls kneaded with straw is the common material of the walls; these are rarely above seven feet high ... they are about two feet thick and have only a door, which lets in light instead of a window, and should let the smoak[13] out instead of a chimney ... The roofs of the cabbins are rafters, raised from the tops of the mud walls, and the covering varies; some are thatched with straw, potato stalks, or with heath, others only covered with sods of turf cut from the grass field.[14]

When Dr Pococke travelled through the north west of Ireland in 1752 he too noted the absence of windows in the dwelling houses. He also observed that the houses had two door openings and not one:

> They have in these parts two doors to their Cabbins, keeping one only open on the side that is not exposed to the wind, as they have no light commonly, only that by the door.[15]

A poetic account of the houses in the west of Ireland in 1676 outlines how this two-door system operated:

> Each cabbin with two Dores is graced,
> Like squirrills 'gainst each other placed.
> One still is stopp'd with Straw and Wattle,
> When wind on that side Howse doth rattle,
> And when to th'other it is shifted,
> The Dore to the other side is lifted.[16]

When Edward Wakefield travelled through Leitrim in August 1809, he too reported that 'the cabin doors were of wattle work, covered on the inside with a straw mat'.[17] The various traveller's accounts help us to build up a picture of these impoverished houses. These written accounts would have been much richer source material if they had been accompanied by sketches[18] or photographs – had photography been developed at that time. It is obvious from all the accounts that one-roomed houses were very common in Leitrim at the beginning of the 19th century and that generally the quality of housing was quite wretched. Yet some improvements were being made. James McParlan, in his detailed report on Co. Leitrim in 1802, stated that 'those hovels [one-roomed houses] are getting fewer by degrees' and that 'chimneys, partitions and separate cow houses were becoming more common'.[19]

McParlan's report at the beginning of the 19th century suggests that some improvements in housing conditions were taking place. However, factors such as the increasing population, the poor and mostly unproductive land and the lack of resident landlords all worked against the prosperity of the people. In 1810, when Robert Lloyd Jones took on to act as a middleman for John King, a local landlord who owned ten townlands bordering the parish of Kiltubrid, he had little idea of the difficulties that would face him.[20] Seven years later he complained to the landlord that

> instead of reaping any benefit by all my exertions I was obliged to give up my time and my health and under a heavy dayly burden of expence in a mud wall smokey cabbin endeavouring to wring rents from bankrupt tenants.[21]

The consecutive bad summers of 1816 and 1817, together with the fever which was rampant in south Leitrim at this time,[22] reduced the tenantry to the point of starvation. Five years later the situation was no better. Lloyd Jones wrote 'Whenever I asked them [the tenants] for rent they called on me for bread and I know they wanted it.'[23] The link between a depressed local agricultural economy and poor housing is suggested by Robert Graham who travelled from Drumsna to Ballinamore and on to Swanlinbar on 30 September 1835. He wrote 'the cottages [are] small and shabby, and the agriculture bad.'[24]

The poverty was crippling and the conditions were not right for improving their living accommodation. The Revd John Maguire, the parish priest of Kiltubrid, reported in 1836 that the houses in his parish were 'of a bad description, badly thatched and badly supplied with bedsteads and bedding.'[25] The descriptions of the houses by Owen McGreal and the Revd M. Heslin from the neighbouring parish of Kiltoghert are more detailed. They reported that the houses were built of mud, bog sods or clay and stones. Owen McGreal said that these houses had 'no shutters or glass to the windows, but [were] occasionally stuffed with straw or rushes, a bundle or flake made of rods for closing the door.'[26] The Revd Heslin outlined the furnishing inside:

> a few stools, some utensils to prepare their food, and a few noggins to drink out of ... The bedding is miserable, consisting in some seasons of straw and hay, in other seasons of green rushes, in most cases there is no covering except the almost worn cloak of the mother or the big coat of the father.[27]

Dr John Dukes had a dispensary in Mohill and was in charge of the fever hospital there. He visited the houses of the labourers 'where no gentleman would go in' and his description in 1844 of the living conditions bears out the evidence of Owen McGreal and the Revd M. Heslin eight years earlier:

> They have no bedstead; they are lying on a small quantity of straw – sometimes rushes; they have no covering over them or one blanket among six. When fever sets in, in any particular case, generally the whole family take it ... Some means should be devised to prevent the people lying on the ground, with no more straw than you could put in your hand.[28]

It seems safe to conclude that as the population continued to grow in the first half of the 19th century so too did the number of houses. The poor and overcrowded houses resulted in their inhabitants being susceptible to disease. Thus the Famine dramatically reduced the number of people and the poorest of the houses were virtually wiped out.

The Famine greatly reduced the number of houses in the parish. However some of the people were homeless before the worst of the Famine set in. On 16 December 1847 Captain Edward Wynne[29] reported that the Carrick-on-Shannon Poor Law Union, which included the parish of Kiltubrid, 'presents peculiar difficulties; vast numbers of families have been unhoused and their houses destroyed.'[30] He spelled out the problem of homelessness in the Carrick-on-Shannon Union:

> I have met a greater amount of urgent and pressing destitution in this Union than in any other part of Ireland I have visited. As in addition to want of food, which exists to a great extent as in any other part of Ireland, want of shelter from the inclemency of the seasons exists to a far greater extent than in any other part with which I am acquainted.[31]

There was a 21.4 per cent drop in the number of houses of all classes in Kiltubrid between the years 1841 and 1851.[32] However, the picture varies greatly from townland to townland within the parish (fig. 2.2). Fourteen townlands, including Laheen, the residence of Richard Reynolds Peyton and Drumineigh Glebe, where the Church of Ireland rectory was, retained all their houses during the worst years of the Famine. The village of Keshcarrigan lost only one house during this period, reducing from 21 to 20 in number. Seven other townlands actually recorded an increase in the number of houses during the decade of the Great Famine, including Aughakilbrack which stretches to the top of Slieve an Iarainn mountain. Two clusters of townlands, one in the north of the parish and one in the south, recorded the biggest reduction of all. The townland of Drumparsons dropped from having ten houses in 1841 to having only one in 1851, and the adjoining townland of Edenmore reduced from having seven houses to just one in the same period. The two adjoining mountain townlands of Gortnawan and Mullagarve lost the greatest number of houses during the Famine years. Between them they lost 41 houses. The only known Famine burial ground in the parish is in the townland of Mullagarve.

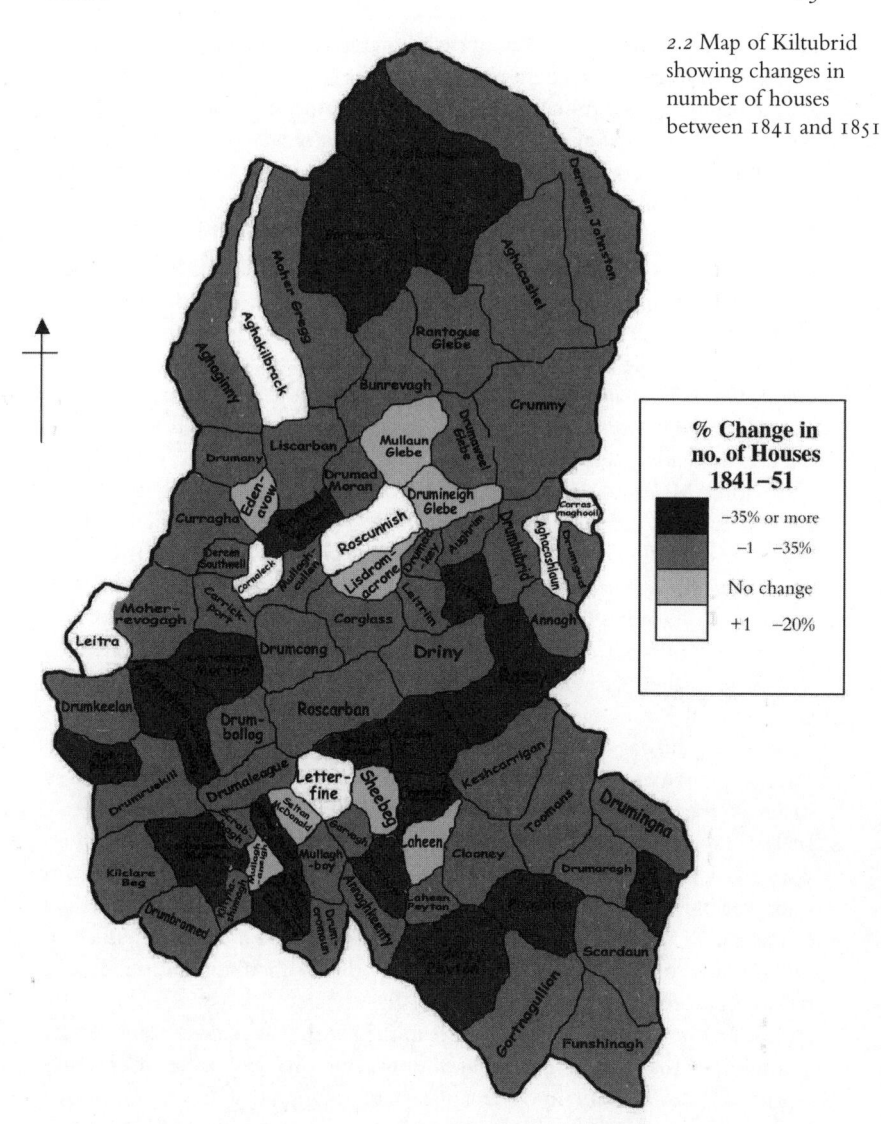

Houses

2.2 Map of Kiltubrid showing changes in number of houses between 1841 and 1851

% Change in no. of Houses 1841–51
−35% or more
−1 −35%
No change
+1 −20%

It is clear that the percentage change in the number of houses in the Famine years varied greatly from townland to townland within the parish of Kiltubrid. The number of houses in Drumparsons dropped by 90 per cent while the number in Corrasmoghaoil increased by 20 per cent. The other 80 townlands in the parish were somewhere in between. For example in the townland of Mullaghgarve, one of the townlands which stretches to the top of Slieve an Iarainn mountain, the average holding was a relatively high 17.4 acres but its Poor Law Valuation was only 1s. 7d. per acre. The unproductive land rather than the average size of each holding contributed to Mullaghgarve losing 20 of its 48 houses between 1841 and 1851.

The land was marginally better in the townland of Corderry Peyton where the Poor Law Valuation was fixed at 5s. 6d. an acre. The average size of each holding was only 8.6 acres and this townland lost 22 of its 43 houses during the Famine years.[33] The value of the land in the townland of Drumparsons was typical for the parish being valued at 6s. 7d. per acre, but here the average size of each holding was only 5.5 acres. This townland lost nine of its ten houses in the Famine years.[34] A telling comparison can be made between Drumparsons and the nearby townland of Garvagh where the average size of holding was somewhat larger at 8.5 acres. The land in Garvagh was a great deal better than that in Drumparsons being valued at 10s. 2d. an acre, and the number of houses remained static in this townland during the worst years of the Famine.

Fr John Maguire, the parish priest of Kiltubrid, stated in 1836 that in general the size of holding in his parish was ten acres, which tenants generally held directly from the head landlord.[35] However lakes, mountain and bog made up much of the land. Many of the labourers had no land at all or else a small garden of no value. In 1856, almost a decade after the worst of the Famine, 13.7 per cent of the houses in Kiltubrid had less than one acre of land. A further 9.5 per cent had less than five acres of land. A total of 45.1 per cent of the holdings were ten acres or under.

It would appear that the size of the holding and the quality of the land were the two most important factors in determining whether a house survived the Great Famine or not. The building of the Ballinamore – Ballyconnell Canal as a famine relief work scheme may have helped those who lived in the townlands nearest to it, since the greatest reduction in houses happened in the townlands farthest away from the canal at the edges of the parish.[36] What is certain is that the Famine had a dramatic effect on the number of houses in the parish and this reduction continued, at a reduced rate, for the rest of the century (fig. 2.3).

It wasn't only the number of houses in the parish that changed dramatically as a result of the Famine. The type of house also changed. James McParlan's report on Co. Leitrim in 1802 appears to suggest that the one-roomed houses were disappearing. Yet in 1841 a total of 43.2 per cent of the houses in the county were still one-roomed.[37] These were the houses in which the poorest labourers lived and these were the houses which were hit hardest during the years of the Great Famine.

One-roomed houses in Leitrim were not completely wiped out by the Famine, but they were dramatically reduced from 43.2 per cent to 15.9 per cent of the total in the ten-year period from 1841 to 1851.[38] This reduction continued during the next half century until they had virtually disappeared by 1901.

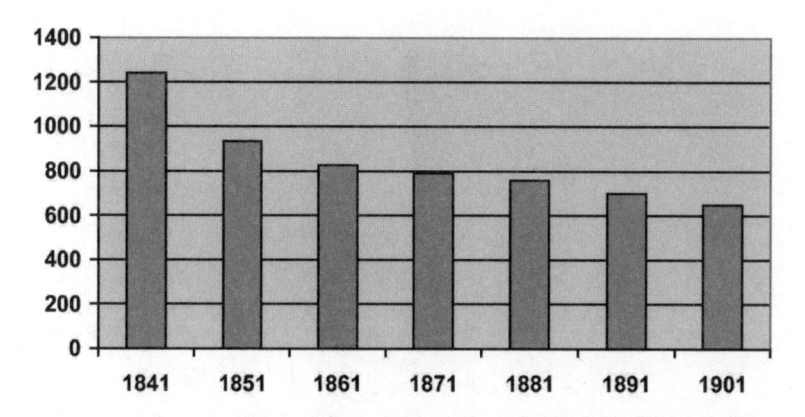

2.3 Total number of houses in Kiltubrid at ten-year intervals between 1841 and 1901

The parish of Kiltubrid, even though much of the land is poor quality bog and mountain land, had only 30.2 per cent of its houses one-roomed in 1841, considerably less than the percentage for the whole county.[39] In 1901 a total of 1.8 per cent of the houses in the parish were one-roomed which was fractionally higher than that for the whole county.[40] However, the same pattern of a dramatic reduction in the number of one-roomed houses after the Famine can be found in Kiltubrid as in much of the west of Ireland.[41] Dr John Duke's observation in 1845 that because of the overcrowded and impoverished conditions people were living in 'when fever sets in, in any

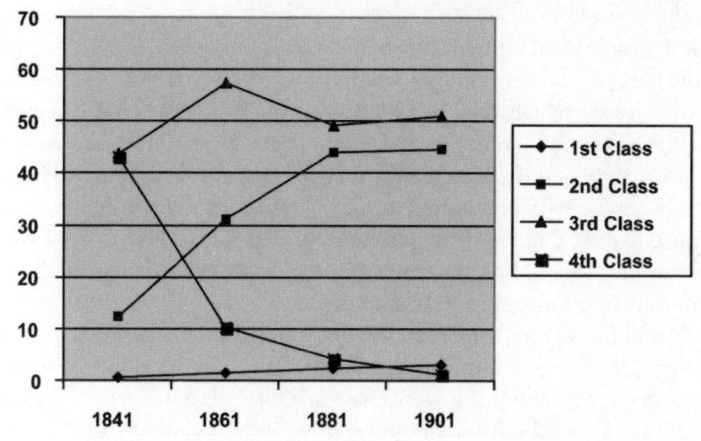

2.4 The percentage of houses in each class in Co. Leitrim at twenty-year intervals between 1841 and 1901

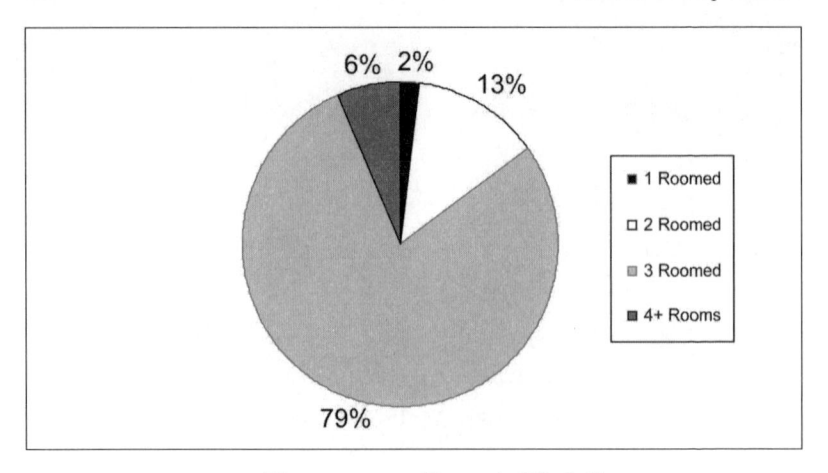

2.5 The percentage of houses in Kiltubrid
with the different number of rooms in 1901

particular case, generally the whole family take it'[42] helps us to understand why so many of the one-roomed houses disappeared at this time. This large reduction in the number of one-roomed houses which continued after the Famine would suggest that they had become associated in people's minds with poverty, famine and disease. Gradually they became a thing of the past.

Even though the one-roomed houses were disappearing rapidly in the decades after the Famine there were still some one-roomed houses being built in this period. A good example of these post-Famine one-roomed houses is Thomas Bearer's house which was built c.1865 near the village of Keshcarrigan.[43] He was a cattle herd and both he and his wife, Catherine, were natives of Co. Galway.[44]

It appears that they built this one-roomed house when they first settled in the area and as their family grew in size they moved out of it to a three-roomed house which they had built nearby.[45] When the roof collapsed on this three-roomed house in the 1930s Kate Bearer, the last remaining member of the family, moved back into the one-roomed house (which had been re-roofed with corrugated iron). She remained there until her death on 2 April 1949.[46] This one-roomed house was not long and narrow like the pre-Famine houses but was built with mortar and good stone and was almost square measuring 4.12 x 3.92 metres.[47]

This house is very similar to the one studied by Alan Gailey in Meenagarragh, Co. Tyrone.[48] Similar type houses are to be found at Ballycronan, Co. Antrim, and along the west coast in Donegal and Kerry.[49] Very often these houses were built for labourers, fishermen or cattle herds.[50] It appears that the house of Thomas Cowan, who lived in the townland of Edenavow, was similar to this one. He was also a cattle-herd and was a native of Co.

Roscommon.[51] These houses bear little resemblance to the pre-Famine one-roomed houses. These post-Famine one-roomed houses were well-built houses and were a smaller version of the three-roomed houses popular in the area in mid-Victorian times.

However, most of the one-roomed houses in the parish in 1901 were of the pre-Famine type. James Shanley lived in a thatched one-roomed house in the townland of Drumany. The house had no windows. He was 70 years old, was not married and he could not read or write. He was a farm labourer.[52] John Flanagan and his sister Mary lived in a mud-walled one roomed house in the townland of Drumaragh. He was 66 years old and his sister was 80 years of age. They were both getting outdoor relief.[53] The people who lived in these one-roomed houses in the parish in 1901 tended to be elderly, single and unskilled. As they died out the one-roomed houses died out with them. And yet some of the one-roomed houses survived well into the 20th century. Pat Curran who lived in Drumcrumaun recorded in 1938 that:

> An old man lived in a very small house ... The house consisted of one room. He kept his bed in the corner beside the fire. The smoke went out through a hole in the roof as there was no chimney. There was an old creamery can in which there was no bottom ... for a chimney.'[54]

The trend is an obvious one. The one-roomed houses were disappearing rapidly and it appears that Kate Bearer, who died in 1949, was the last person in the parish to live in one of these one-roomed houses. By then they had become a thing of the past.

The Famine set in motion many changes in housing in Kiltubrid. Certain patterns emerge. The total number of houses began to decrease. There was a move from one-roomed houses to three-roomed houses (fig. 2.4). There was a move also from mud-walled houses to substantial stone-walled, mortared houses. With this development the houses changed from being hip-roofed to being gabled houses. The wattle and straw doors were replaced with wooden doors, both full and half doors.[55] There was a new tendency to whitewash the stone-walled houses for hygienic and health reasons as well as for aesthetic ones.[56] Slates had become more common in parts of Ulster, particularly in counties Antrim and Down in the 17th century but it was not until the second half of the 19th century that they became common in south Ulster.[57] Slated roofs were still quite rare in Kiltubrid with only 4.9 per cent of the houses being slated in 1901.[58]

Despite the failure of the agricultural economy to pick up in much of the west of Ireland, the decades after the Famine saw considerable improvement in the standard of housing there. So the trend is an obvious one. There was a move throughout the 19th century towards better housing. This change was accelerated by the Great Famine in the middle of the century. By the 1890s the standard of housing in Kiltubrid had improved considerably from the

2.6 An Irish cottage of the worst kind, August 1889

beginning of the century. Henry Doran, in his report to the Congested Districts Board for the district[59] of Kiltubrid, stated in 1895 that:

> The dwellings as a rule are substantially built with stone walls (about seven feet high to eave) and mortar, and contain a kitchen and two rooms. The roofs are thatched, oats or rye straw being used for the outer covering by all who can provide it. Those who have not straw use rushes or long heath.[60]

He added that 120 (10.2 per cent) of the families lived in 'very poor circumstances.'[61] The fact that some people lived in very poor housing is best illustrated by Leland Duncan's 1889 photograph of what he called 'an Irish cabin of the worst kind'[62] (fig. 2.6).

This photograph, perhaps more than any others taken by Duncan, demonstrates the importance of photographs for the study of local history. No written account, no matter how detailed it was, could capture the impoverished living conditions depicted here in the graphic way that these photographs do. E. Estyn Evans draws a distinction between sod and turf houses and this house would seem to fit into the latter category.[63] It was not uncommon for the corners or end walls of these houses to collapse under the weight of the roof as this one has done.[64] The wooden central hearth chimney, the two irregular sized windows and the grass tufts on the thatch all suggest neglect and poverty.

Duncan took two photographs of this house. His second photograph, the one taken from the good end of the house, would indicate that this house was, at one time, a well-built turf house with rounded corners and neatly pinned thatch.⁶⁵ These photographs taken by Leland L. Duncan in 1889, tell us loudly and clearly that not all of the poor housing disappeared in the Famine years and that some very poor housing still existed forty years after the worst of the Great Famine was over.

By the end of the year 1900 there were 12 (1.8 per cent of the total) mud-walled houses in the parish of Kiltubrid. These houses were to be found mostly in the northern townlands on Slieve-an-Iarainn mountain or to the east of the parish where the soil was mostly peaty and the land poor. It is notable that there were virtually no mud-walled, one-roomed or two-roomed houses in the townlands to the south and west of the parish where the land was more fertile and where a better network of roads existed than elsewhere in the parish. There was a direct correlation between the quality of the land and the quality of the houses (fig. 2.7). The type and size of the mud-walled houses varied considerably. Patrick Gallagher lived in the townland of Edenavow in a mud-walled house with two rooms and two windows – much like the house photographed by Leland L. Duncan.

John Rorke, a 72-year-old labourer, lived in the townland of Drumingna. His house was the worst in the parish, being mud-walled, one-roomed, thatched and without any windows. Usually there were only one or two occupants in the mud-walled houses, though Ellen McElroy lived with her five children in a mud-walled house in Dereen Johnston and Thomas McWeeney lived with four others in a mud walled house in Leitra. Some of the mud-walled houses were three-roomed. Pat McGovern lived in the townland of Aughaginny with his two sisters, Jane and Margaret, in a mud-walled house with three rooms and windows.⁶⁶ Most of the occupants of the mud-walled houses were elderly and the mud-walled houses died out with them.

The one-roomed and mud-walled houses were almost, but not quite, extinct in the parish by 1901. Two-roomed houses were much more common. There were 84 (13 per cent of the total) two-roomed houses in the parish at the end of the 19th century. The two-roomed houses were to be found mostly in the north and east of the parish, where the land was wet, peaty or mountainous. The townland of Crummy had the highest ratio of two-roomed houses in the parish with nine of its 27 houses being two-roomed. The land in this townland was mostly bog land. The townland of Leitra, a townland with poor quality land to the south and west of the parish, bears out this link between the quality of the land and the type of housing. Five of the eight houses in this townland were of poor quality, with three of them being two-roomed. There were no poor houses in any of the neighbouring townlands that had good quality limestone land.

Leitrim had relatively few big houses or great estates. In 1901 only 6.3 per cent of the houses in Kiltubrid had four or more rooms.⁶⁷ In 1837 Samuel Lewis listed five big houses in the parish of Kiltubrid – Reynolds of

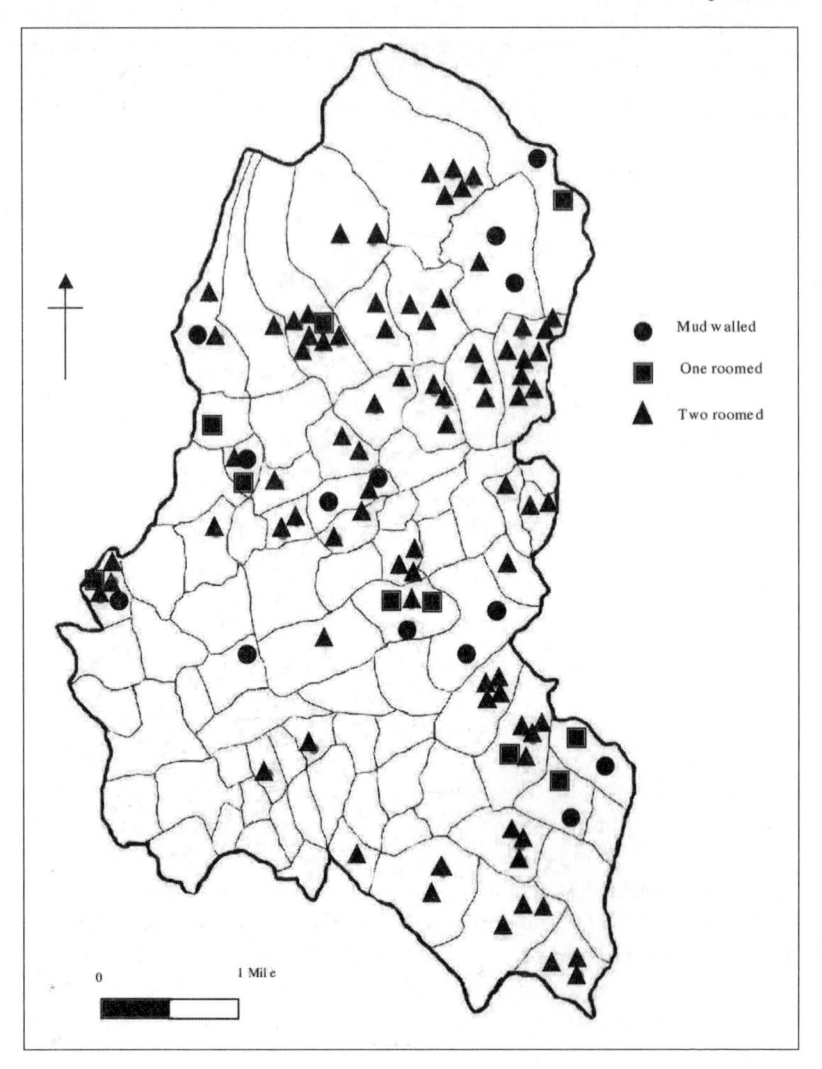

2.7 Map of Kiltubrid showing the distribution of the poorest houses in 1901

Lough Scur (Letterfine), Peytons of Laheen, Slackes of Annadale, Peytons of Driney and Johnstons of Aughacashel.[68] These were small estates with none having more than five hundred acres. None of them were walled estates. The big houses, mirroring the size of the estates, were all modestly sized. By the 1890s the Reynolds were gone from Letterfine, and the Peytons from Laheen. The Johnstons were gone from Aughacashel House and it was owned by James Maguire, who was said to be in 'a very delicate state of health, and anxious to dispose of the place.'[69] Aughacashel House and Driney House

2.8 Laheen House, c. 1899

were substantial 18th century three storied houses.[70] Annadale House, the home of James Wilkinson Slacke and his family, was a two-storied slated house with two chimneys. It had a large doorway and nine windows on the front wall.[71] Letterfine House, which had been the residence of the Reynolds family of Loughscur, was a 17th century thatched house, but was, by the 1890s, vacant and falling into disrepair.[72]

Laheen House, was a large traditional thatched mansion type house (fig. 2.8). It had been the home the Peyton family but was, during the 1890s, occupied by the Barrett family. It was a 17th-century two-storied vernacular house with four chimneys and gabled ends. It had a doorway and ten windows in the front wall and had fourteen rooms inside[73] In many ways Laheen House is the most interesting of the big houses in the parish at this period since it is the oldest and is vernacular in style.[74] The proportions seem to be the same as the much smaller three-roomed houses which were so popular in the area at this time. This suggests that the three-roomed thatched houses which became widespread in the post-Famine years were modelled on the early big house model.[75] The photograph of Laheen House and Leland Duncan's photograph of Driney House (see fig. 2.9) spell out the importance of photographs for historical research since the former was burned in 1911 and the latter in 1920.

The rectory in Drumineigh Glebe was erected in 1825 with the aid of a loan of £530 from the Board of First Fruits.[76] It was a large slated house with fourteen rooms and five windows facing the front.[77] The parish priest's house, built in 1878, was also a substantial two storey house with ten rooms and five windows in front.[78] The big houses in Kiltubrid, when compared

2.9 Driney House, August 1889

with those in other parts of Ireland, were not really big houses at all. Yet the photographs of Leland L. Duncan capture the great disparity that existed between the biggest and the smallest houses, the best ones and the worst ones, in the parish.

When researching Laheen House I knew, from the 1837 Ordnance Survey map, where it was situated and that it was L-shaped.[79] I learned from the 1901 Census of Ireland that there were 14 rooms in it, that it was thatched and had ten windows in front. But I still did not know what it looked like. This photograph, which I tracked down in Chicago after fifteen years of searching, shows how persistence can be rewarded. The photograph complements the other sources and completes the picture.[80]

Throughout the 19th century there was a marked improvement in the quality of housing in Ireland. In general the move was one from fourth class to second class housing, from one-roomed houses to three-roomed ones that were built with better quality materials. The poorer houses disappeared much more quickly in the east of the country than elsewhere and by the end of the century they survived mainly along the west coast.[81] The parish of Kiltubrid had seen a marked improvement in its standard of housing as the 19th century progressed and yet this 'congested district' had still some very poor housing at the end of the century.

2. Land

Most of the accounts of farming in Co. Leitrim in the pre-Famine years describe not just the poor, wet and unproductive land and the high rainfall but also the primitive farming practices employed by the people there. The 30-year period after the great Famine was, with the exception of the years 1859 to 1864, a time of prosperity and growth for Irish farming. The change from arable farming to pastoral farming, which had begun before the Famine, accelerated in this 30 year period and contributed to the prosperity.[1] However, the growth in prosperity was not uniform throughout Ireland. In Leitrim, and much of the north west of Ireland, farming remained in a pre-Famine mode with farming practices remaining largely unchanged throughout the 19th century.[2] In this chapter we examine the agricultural economy of Kiltubrid in the 1890s, the farming methods practiced, the outhouses that existed and the attempts by the tenant farmers to establish a 'system of peasant proprietary.'[3]

Leland L. Duncan kept a pocket diary during his 1892 visit to Kiltubrid.[4] The diary begins on Friday 5 August 1892 as he leaves London for Ireland and ends on Tuesday 6 September when he returned to work in the War Office. This diary complements the photographs he took during that visit and makes many references to the farming practices of the people of Kiltubrid at that time. 'Morning fine,' he wrote on 12 August 1892, 'and we got the best of the hay cocked,' [on the Annadale estate] despite the weather being 'unsettled'.[5] The picture one gets from the diary is of a smash and grab operation where they managed to save some hay despite the vagaries of the weather. However, this entry also suggests poor farming practice because if the hay was to be of good quality it should have been cut and saved much earlier in the summer.

The late saving of hay in Leitrim was raised by Revd Charles Clarke in 1836 when he complained that

> these lands are pastured to so late a period (mostly to the latter end of May) that a large portion of them are not fit for mowing until after the harvest has been secured …[6]

He outlined how the farm practices in the area were so backward that Mr Fox, on his estate at Dromahair, offered several prizes to his tenants to improve their farming methods. These included a prize for 'the saving of hay and securing it in the haggard prior to the 1st August.'[7]

The efforts of Fox and others to improve the hay-making habits in Leitrim had little effect and not much had changed by the 1890s. In 1891 it was reported that, while generally hay yields in Leitrim were down, 'some of it which was cut early is exceptionally well saved, and the remainder is badly saved.'[8] The weather during the months of May and June of that year was particularly dry. Yet the tenant farmers had not saved their hay early because they had grazed their cattle on the meadows 'as there was no grass on the pasture lands which caused the meadows to be late and light.'[9]

Edward Wakefield travelled through Leitrim in the month of August 1809. He too reported that the people were busily employed making hay.[10] He did not comment on the late harvesting of the hay but he did note that the people were 'tossing the hay about with their hands; and had no idea that this operation could be better performed with a fork.'[11] McParlan's report at the beginning of the 1800s stated that the farm tools in use in Leitrim were 'plough, loy, shovel, spade, grape, pitchfork, slane, harrow, rake, fork and steeven.'[12] However, it appears that the use of these tools was not widespread in the county.[13] By 1836 it was reported that English tools were gradually being introduced into the county and that these were more efficient than those usually employed in the area.[14] The farming methods were basic and crude not just for saving the hay but also for bringing it in for winter storage. The Revd Charles Clarke reported in 1836 that

> it is not an unfrequent [sic] occurrence to see six or seven persons, of both sexes and all ages, engaged in carrying on their backs the corn and hay from the field to the haggard.[15]

Henry Doran, in his report to the Congested Districts Board, had nothing to say about the practise of haymaking in Kiltubrid in the mid 1890s though he did make the comment that 'as a rule, the hay is coarse, and of inferior quality'.[16] Part of the problem was that the meadows were never re-seeded to improve the quality of the hay (table 3.1).

Leland L. Duncan's 1892 pocket diary is useful as a primary source for studying the farming practices of this period. However, the photographs he took between 1889 and 1894 are much more useful in this respect. His photograph of the meitheal building the hay-rick in August 1894 would suggest that hay-making practices had improved since the pre-Famine years and that hay-making tools were now more widely used (fig. 3.1).

Duncan uses the photograph in figure 3.1 to depict, not just the men who were building the rick, but also the pitchforks they were using. The pitchforks included one extra-long handled one for pitching the hay when the rick got high. The picture also shows the horse which dragged or 'snigged' the hay into the haggard.

Duncan photographed a second rick-building meitheal during his 1894 visit. This photograph shows a rick of hay shaped and raked with one of the

3.1 Meitheal building hay-rick, August 1894

men holding a wooden hay-rake that was used to comb down and finish off the surface of the hayrick.[17] This farm tool had been omitted from the other meitheal photograph shown in figure 3.1. In August 1892 he took a snapshot of Mikey Lynch holding a sickle that he was using to trim the cypress trees at Annadale.[18] Duncan had deliberately placed farm tools against the wall of McManus's house before he photographed it in August 1894 (fig. 2.1). He wasn't satisfied that this photograph showed off the tools well enough and so he took another photograph of them, this time from close range (fig. 3.2). In this way Duncan systematically photographed the farm tools being used in the area.

The sleán, steveen and loy, depicted here were all made locally by combining the skills of a blacksmith and carpenter. The sleán was used in much of Ireland for cutting turf though the instrument varied from place to place.[19] The steveen and the loy were farm tools peculiar to Co. Leitrim, west Cavan and south Fermanagh.[20] The loy was an extra heavy spade which was used to dig lazy beds or ridges for the potatoes and the steveen was an all wooden tool used to dibble or make holes in the ridges to drop the potato seeds into. This process was known locally as 'gogaring'.[21]

Photographs can also be used for comparative purposes. Leland L. Duncan's photographs can usefully be compared with those of William Fee McKinney (1832–1917), who was trying to build up a photographic record of farming practices near Carnmoney in Co. Antrim at the same time Duncan was doing so in Co. Leitrim.[22] Both made a valiant attempt to

3.2 Some farm tools used in Kiltubrid in the 1890s, August 1894

record with camera the farm implements used in these counties. What strikes one immediately is that the farming practices in the north east of the country were so much more advanced than those in Co. Leitrim. William McKinney's photographs show agricultural practices that were centred around the horse and horse-drawn machines. Duncan's photographs, on the other hand, show the hand-tools used for farm work in Leitrim. William McKinney photographed a swing-plough, several horse carts, a reaping machine, roller, horse drawn hay-rake and rick-shifter.[23] The agricultural economy in Antrim was horse centred in the 1890s. In Leitrim it was not.

James McParlan reported at the beginning of the 1800s that the people of Leitrim 'complain of a scarcity of horses,' that they seldom use a plough and that 'the mode of [agri]culture is with a long narrow spade commonly called a loy.'[24] Seven years later Edward Wakefield wrote that horses were still a rarity in Leitrim and that the harness on the horses that were there 'was very rude ... it was merely a hay or straw rope or band.'[25] He did meet a group of people on horseback going to a wedding but said that 'on inquiry I found that they were all Protestants.'[26] This scarcity of horses in Leitrim at this period is in stark contrast to the poor Scottish highland parish of Morvern which had 100 breeding mares and 150 working horses a decade earlier than this.[27] Horses were still scarce in Leitrim three decades later. Charles Clarke stated in 1836 that:

> The small number of horses which are kept by the farmers ... is a
> subject that demands notice ... Their places are mostly kept by asses of
> which many are kept ... The parish priest of Cloone states that, on his
> neighbours assisting him in drawing his turf during the last summer, out
> of 38 animals so employed there were only two horses and 36 asses.[28]

The situation was largely unchanged sixty years later. Henry Doran wrote that:

> The number of horses in this district [Kiltubrid] is small. The small
> landholders do not keep horses, but all have donkeys, which would be
> much improved in size and strength by crossing with the smallest class
> of Spanish stallion asses.[29]

Donkeys were much easier and much less expensive to keep than horses. Asses, unlike horses, could survive outdoors in winter on relatively poor land. The horse, being a heavier animal, was less suited to wet land and required oats to supplement the grass and hay it consumed. It was estimated that it cost approximately £8 to buy a horse and another £8 per year to keep one in the 1890s which was a considerable sum considering that the average income for families in Kiltubrid was estimated at less than £35 per year.[30] The horse was a luxury most tenant farmers in the area could not afford.

On Wednesday 17 August 1894 Leland L. Duncan wrote in his diary, 'Day fine and bright, I did some photos of the asses and men in the bog – turf carrying'.[31] The photographs he took show asses, without any head harness, with creels on their backs carrying home the turf.[32] Duncan took several photographs of horses, one depicting Dr Little, the local medical doctor, with his two horses drawing a fine back-to-back carriage.[33] The Revd Hoops, Church of Ireland rector of Fenagh, had a less elaborate side-car which was drawn by one horse.[34] Another photograph shows Thomas, the servant man in the back yard at Annadale, with the horse saddled in readiness for his master.[35] The only photograph of a horse involved directly in farm work is that shown in fig. 3.1. Yet we must be careful about drawing conclusions from photographic sources. We cannot generalise or quantify from them. Perhaps our best guide to the number of horses in the parish is that according to the 1901 census 12.5 per cent of the households in the parish had stables, 2 per cent had coach houses and 0.3 per cent had the luxury of a harness shed.[36]

The amount of farm machinery, especially mowing, reaping and threshing machines, increased considerably in Ireland between 1865 and 1890.[37] This increase did not happen in Leitrim and the scarcity of horses to draw this machinery was still evident at the end of the century. Because of the scarcity of horses in Kiltubrid Henry Doran reported that 'the land is chiefly cultivated by manual labour.'[38] The loy was their plough, the scythe their mower and the flail their thresher. The absence of horses, ploughs and other horse-drawn farm machinery restricted the development and growth of agriculture in the area.

In 1802 James McParlan referred to the soil in Leitrim as being 'stiff, heavy, cold' and 'very retentive of water.'[39] He advocated land drainage as a solution.[40] By 1845 little drainage had been done. Arthur John Vesey Burchell, who lived at Blackrock house, near Drumshanbo, reported in that year that 'agriculture [in Leitrim] is much neglected and the lands want draining.'[41] Leland L. Duncan noted in his diary on 24 August 1892 that the men on the Annadale estate were busy 'opening a bog drain.' However, this was the exception rather than the rule and two years later Henry Doran, in his report to the Congested Districts Board, deplored the fact that:

> The people [of Kiltubrid] work hard for three-fourths of the year, but they are practically idle from November to February. Even those who could employ their leisure time to great advantage in the drainage and improvement of their lands make no effort to do so during the winter months.[42]

One of Henry Doran's main recommendations for improving the agriculture in Kiltubrid was 'to induce the people to drain [the land], with covered stone drains.'[43] The land was wet and badly in need of drainage. Virtually no progress had been made in this respect throughout the 19th century.

In other respects too the farming methods in Leitrim were backward and detrimental to the soil. In the pre-Famine decades it was common practice to grow potatoes on the same patch of land for two consecutive years and then to continue to sow oats on that same patch year after year until the soil was exhausted. The land was then left waste until it gradually recovered by natural means.[44] During the early decades of the 19th century there was very little manure to fertilize the land since there were few cow-sheds and little fodder and most cattle were wintered outside. The land was burned regularly to clear it and to fertilise it:

> Animal manure and lime are much used on the mountain lands and also for reclaiming the bogs. Burning prevails to a very great extent, and several of the small farmers have no other means of manure, and almost all occupiers burn more or less every year.[45]

Dr John Dukes, the medical doctor in Mohill, stated that the small farmers used 'cow manure with a quantity of lime mixed with mud' as a fertilizer, but that the 'poor have no manures, except by burnings which is carried out to a great extent.'[46] Fr George Gearty, parish priest of Annaduff, stated that the potatoes the people depended on for survival were all 'lumpers … of the very worst description'[47] because the soil was too impoverished. There were a few attempts at improving the farming practices in the pre-Famine years most notably on the Fox estate in Dromahair[48] and on Lord Leitrim's estate near Mohill, where agriculturists had been employed and tenants were encouraged to grow green crops.[49] Despite these efforts not much progress was made in trying to persuade the tenant farmers to diversify their crops and little green crops were being sown by the end of the century in the Kiltubrid district (table 3.1).

Table 3.1 Average quantity of land in statute acres used for various purposes in Kiltubrid in 1894 on holdings of about £4 valuation

	A.	R.	P.
Oats	0	3	0
Potatoes	1	1	0
Green crops including cabbage	0	0	30
Permanent meadow	4	0	0
Meadow grown from grass seeds	0	0	0

Source: Henry Doran, Base Line Report to Congested Districts Board, in James Morrissey (ed.), *On the verge of want* (Dublin, 2001), p. 67.

In general, the poor farming methods employed in Leitrim before the Famine continued after it. By the middle of the 1890s the same basic problems existed in Kiltubrid. Henry Doran reported that:

> No rotation of crops is followed. The only crops grown are potatoes, oats, rye, and a plot of cabbage. Very few people grow even a small plot of turnips ... Artificial manure is not used. The only manure used is that made on the farm, which in the case of the small landholders having little or no stock, is largely composed of rushes, heath, and coarse grass placed in cesspools to rot and afterwards mixed with the manure of the livestock. The same plot of ground is frequently kept in cultivation for several years. No grass seeds are sown.[50]

The best aspect of the agricultural economy in Kiltubrid in the 1890s was the quality of the cattle which was said to be superior to that in other congested districts along the western seaboard.

Henry Doran attributed the good breed of cattle to the influence of the neighbouring county of Roscommon where bulls were bought and where the young cattle were sent to the good grazing lands for the summer months. He did say that the cattle were still capable of much improvement and he recommended Polled Angus bulls as the most suitable breed for the area.[51]

Table 3.2 The receipts and expenditure of an average family of six persons, living on a holding in 1894 of about £4 poor law valuation

Receipts	£ s. d.	Expenditure	£ s. d.
Sale of cattle	8 0 0	Indian meal,	5 0 0
Sale of pigs	9 0 0	Flour for family	5 0 0
Sale of butter	4 0 0	Grinding oats	10 0
Sale of eggs	3 10 0	Tea & sugar	2 10 0
Sale of chickens/geese	15 0	American bacon	1 10 0
Savings from family members who are migratory workers in England or Scotland or who have emigrated permanently	8 0 0	Tobacco	1 8 0
		Grazing for cattle	2 10 0
		Cost of 3 young pigs	2 2 0
		Candles/soap etc	1 10 0
		Salt fish	10 0
		Clothes for family	7 0 0
		Rent & county cess	4 5 0
Total:	33 05 0		33 15 0

Source: Morrissey (ed.), *On the verge of want*, p. 70.

The impoverished agricultural economy and the precarious existence the tenant farmers eked out is best captured by table 3.2. Their survival depended on getting an average of £8 per year from family members who had emigrated or who were working as migratory labourers. Kiltubrid in the 1890s was a place where people lived rather than made a living.

Because of the precarious nature of the agricultural economy in Leitrim whenever there was a downturn in agricultural prices or whenever there were bad harvests, as happened in the period 1877 to 1880, the fear of famine was never far away. By the autumn of 1879 a crisis point had been reached. Terence Murray, the parish priest of Carrigallen, spoke at a public meeting in the town and said that the people had no potatoes to live on and that 2,000 cocks of hay were lost because of the flooding in the area.[52] To add to the problems of the tenant farmers of Leitrim the demand for migratory workers had fallen dramatically.[53] Public meetings were held throughout the county calling on the landlords for abatements in rents to relieve the distress.

The killing of Philip Meehan from Coraleehanbeg, near Ballinamore on 14 June 1880 further strengthened the resolve of the tenant farmers.[54] He was one of a large crowd that tried to prevent an evicted farm from being fenced by the landlord Henry B. Acheson. Branches of the Irish National Land League were founded throughout the county during the final months of 1880, including one in Keshcarrigan.[55] Large meetings were held, including one at Proughlish near Keshcarrigan, on 19 September 1880. Five bands led contingents from all over the county to the venue.[56] Jasper Tully, the editor of the *Roscommon Herald*, was the main speaker. Among the locals on the platform were John Rutledge from Keshcarrigan, William Walsh and Thomas Ward from Proughlish and Thomas Moran from Tooman. Thomas Moran proposed a resolution protesting against evictions and pledging not to take farms from which tenants had been evicted. William Walsh proposed that:

> We resolve to use all the means in our power to abolish the system of landlordism which has operated against the peace and happiness and prosperity of the country, and we will regard as the only final solution of the land question the immediate establishment of a system of peasant proprietary.[57]

By the end of the year 1880 agrarian turmoil was spreading in Kiltubrid and in Leitrim. In November of that year, Michael Barrett, bailiff for the absentee landlord Richard Reynolds Peyton, was met by a crowd of 400 people outside Keshcarrigan when he went to collect overdue rents. He was forced to leave without the rent. Later Peyton's cattle were driven off his land at Letterfine and the fences broken down.[58] Another local landlord, Randal Thomas Slacke from Annadale, received a letter, late in the year 1880, threatening him with the fate of Lord Leitrim if he did not 'dale fair' with his tenants.[59]

In the last decade of the 18th century the impoverished people of Leitrim learned how to be subversive and joined such secret societies as the Defenders and the United Irishmen.[60] Now, almost a century later, the tenant farmers were learning how to organise themselves to achieve their aims by mostly legitimate means. The fact that new organisations such as the Irish National League, the Irish National Federation and the Gaelic Athletic Association sprung up in the parish in the period 1880 to 1900 points to a new-found confidence, purpose and sense of direction. It would be almost a decade into the 20th century though before they had their 'system of peasant proprietary.'

Historians are now paying more attention to the built environment than they did in the past. We have much to learn from this approach. By studying farm buildings we can learn much about the agricultural economy of the people, their livestock and their relative wealth or poverty.

Farm buildings were very scarce in Leitrim at the beginning of the 19th century. Many of the dwelling houses gave shelter to the animals as well. James McParlan, writing in 1802, described how it was common for the family and the cows to share the one-roomed dwelling houses.[61] Other travellers' accounts describe how pigs and hens were also sheltered within the dwelling house. McParlan did say that those hovels were gradually disappearing and that chimneys, partitions and separate cow-houses were becoming more common.[62] McParlan's observation proved to be an accurate one because, as we shall see later, most families had one or more out-houses by the end of the 19th century. The built environment in Kiltubrid and in Leitrim changed considerably during the course of the 19th century. The main thrust of this change was from one building, which provided shelter for people and farm

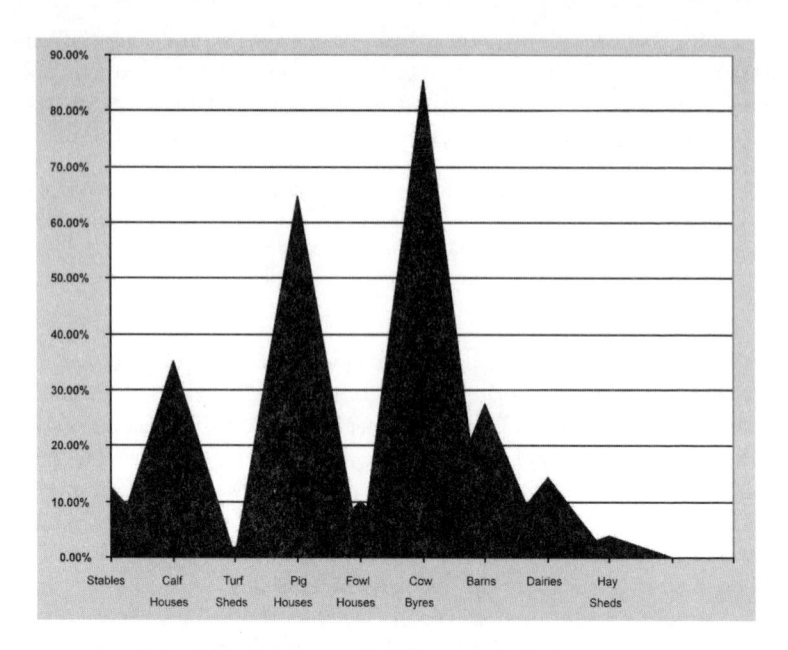

3.3 The percentage of holdings in Kiltubrid in 1901 with the various type of farm buildings

animals, to multiple buildings, and to dwelling houses being divided into rooms and being used, almost exclusively, to give shelter to people.

If the dwelling houses were of poor quality during the 19th century then the outhouses were poorer still. It was reported in 1836 that the cows in Leitrim were 'housed during the winter in close low sheds, very imperfectly built.'[63] In Leitrim most of the outhouses were attached to the end of the dwelling house either in the same line as it, or at right angles to it, forming a half-courtyard.[64] In this way the animals gave heat to the end rooms of the dwelling houses. These outhouses were generally lower than the dwelling houses they were attached to and were built with substantial stone walls and thatched roofs.[65] Some of the outhouses were built parallel to the dwelling house. This type was more common in the townlands of Kiltubrid that were high up on Slieve an Iarainn mountain. When built this way the out-houses not only gave shelter to the animals but also sheltered the dwelling house from the prevailing winds. However, the most common type of outhouses were the extended farmstead and the half-court one.

Henry Doran wrote in 1895 that 'the great majority of the people [in Kiltubrid] have out-offices for their livestock, and very few keep cattle in their dwellings.'[66] The graph in fig. 3.3 bears this out. It shows that in 1901 a total of 85.5 per cent of the households in Kiltubrid had cow byres. When you consider that 15.5 per cent of the holdings in the parish had less than one acre in 1856 then it becomes clear that virtually all households with enough land to graze a cow had a cow-house by the end of the century. The cow was a prized animal and central to the economy of the parish at this time.

Henry Doran estimates that in the 1890s the average annual income per household in the parish of Kiltubrid from cattle was £8 from the sale of two animals and a further £4 from the sale of butter.[67] This amounted to more than one third of the total average annual income for households in the parish. A total of 35.2 per cent of the households had calf-sheds which would suggest that quite a few of the tenant farmers sold off their young stock before the winter set in. Only 14.2 per cent of the houses had dairies even though butter making was an important part of the economy of the area making up approximately one-eighth of the total yearly income. Henry Doran explained that 'There are few dairies [in Kiltubrid], and the milk and butter are usually kept in one of the sleeping rooms.'[68] The cow was the most important animal on the farms and the high percentage of households with cow-byres reflects that.

Richard Griffith's valuation of tenements lists farm-buildings as 'offices' but does not specify what purpose that building or buildings served. The manuscript returns for the Census of Ireland 1901 are much more detailed and consequently much more useful in this matter.

Cattle were plentiful in Kiltubrid in the 1890s and horses were scarce with just 12.5 per cent of householders having a stable. Asses were very plentiful but, unlike horses, they did not require winter shelter and so their big numbers are not reflected in our graph of farm-out-houses. There were no sheds to house sheep in the parish which is not surprising since Henry Doran reported that 'there are very few sheep in the district ... except a small number of people who have sheep on the mountain.[69] The lack of sheep in the district is surprising since the land would seem suitable for them and many other congested districts along the west coast reported considerable numbers of sheep.[70]

The chief corn crops in Leitrim in the 1890s were oats and, to a lesser extent, rye (table 3.3). The high rainfall and wet soil were considered unsuitable conditions for growing wheat or barley. The chief crops grown in the Kiltubrid, as in the rest of Leitrim, at this time were potatoes, oats, rye and plots of cabbage[71] (table 3.1). Potatoes were the chief crop and yet only 0.3 per cent of the households had sheds built specially to house potatoes. The potatoes did not need housing and they were usually clamped in the fields and covered with rushes and sods to keep out the rain and the frost. Oats and rye could be built into stacks and stored in this way before it was threshed. However, once it was threshed it required a dry shed for storage. A total of 27.5 per cent of the houses in the parish had barns to store the grain.[72] Obviously grain was not as important to the economy as the cattle were.

Hay was the main winter fodder for the cattle and horses and yet only 3.9 per cent of the houses in the parish had hay-sheds at this period. William McKinney photographed a hay-shed being built in Co. Antrim by the

Belfast firm of Potts & Houston in the year 1903. The shed cost £52.[73] This price would have been out of reach for most tenant farmers in Kiltubrid whose average annual income in 1895 was not much more than half that amount.[74] Hay-sheds were not essential as the hay could be built into ricks or pikes in the haggard and stored in this way, without much loss, during the winter months.[75] Similarly, but with some loss, turf could be built into clamps and stored out-doors. We mustn't be surprised that only 1.9 per cent of the houses in the parish had turf-sheds in 1901.

Table 3.3 Corn crops in Leitrim, by hundred-weight for the year 1892

Wheat	Oats	Barley	Rye
315	148,883	18	6,215

Source: *Agricultural statistics, Ireland, 1892, produce of the crops*, HC, 1892, lxxxviii, p.10.

Pigs were the most valued animals after the cattle. This is reflected in figure 3.4 which shows that 64.7 per cent of the households in Kiltubrid had pig-houses at this time. Very often these pig-houses were very small with low entrances that required an adult to stoop to gain entry.[76] According to Henry Doran, the sale of pigs brought in an average of £9 annually to each house. This amounted to more than one quarter of the total annual income. Our graph of the farm outhouses in figure 3.4 indicates clearly the importance of pigs to the local economy. Henry Doran suggested that the 'pigs would be much improved ... by crossing with large Yorkshire boars.'[77]

Table 3.4 Green crops by ton weight produced in Leitrim in 1892

Potatoes	Turnips	Cabbage	Flax*	Hay
50,955	15,755	14,088	277	119,801

* Flax is given by stone weight and not ton weight.
Source: *Agricultural statistics, Ireland, 1892, produce of the crops*, H.C., 1892, lxxxviii, p.11.

Henry Doran, in his report to the Congested Districts Board, stated that hens were plentiful but of a poor breed in the area. Hens require shelter, especially at night-time, to protect them from the predatory fox. And yet only 9.9 per cent of the households had fowl-houses at this time. In most instances the cow-byres could also house the hens and keep them sheltered and safe.[78] Henry Doran estimated that the sale of eggs and the sale of chickens and geese brought in, on average, £4 10s. yearly to a typical household in the parish. Fowl were an integral part of the economy, though their importance is not truly reflected in figure 3.4.

The graph of the farm buildings in Kiltubrid does not accurately reflect the importance of asses, fowl, butter or potatoes to the local agricultural

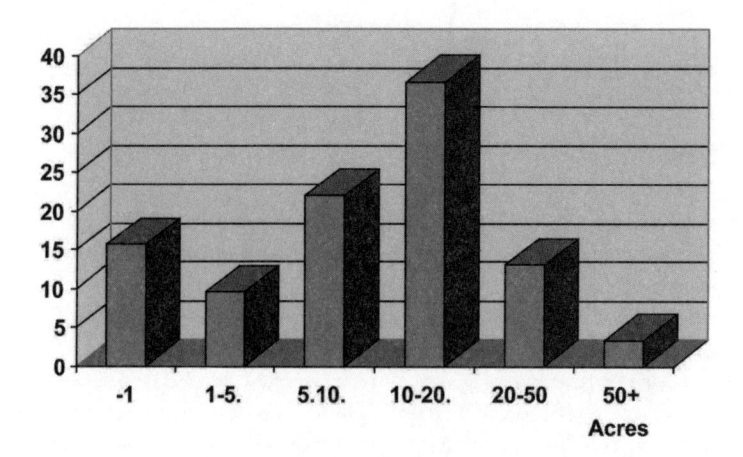

3.4 The percentage of holdings in Kiltubrid
in the various size categories in 1856

economy of the area. But it does give an important insight into the type of farming practiced, the scarcity of horses and the central part played by cattle and pigs in that economy. The variety of outhouses and their prevalence at almost every house also marks a vast improvement on the way things were one hundred years earlier. Major changes had taken place during the 19th century in the built environment. The dwelling houses had improved greatly and there were now, in most cases, little thatched out-houses adjoining them to meet the needs of what was still a fairly primitive agricultural economy.

There were many problems facing the tenant farmers of Kiltubrid in the 1890s. The land was, in general, poor farming land. To outsiders, like James McParlan at the beginning of the nineteenth and Henry Doran at the end of it, there were many obvious improvements that could be made. Both men suggested draining the land, rotating crops, and fertilizing it well. Doran in particular recommended improving the breed of cattle, asses, pigs and poultry. He recommended sowing grass seed and improving the quality of seed potatoes. The tenant farmers themselves saw the landlord system as the main problem which contributed to their impoverished state and they supported the call for a system of 'peasant proprietary'. They agitated for that in the 1880s and the various land acts which were passed gave them hope that they might eventually achieve this. In many instances though the main problem was that the farms were simply too small (fig. 3.4).

Almost half the holdings (47 per cent) were under ten acres in size and 83.6 per cent of the holdings were twenty acres or less in 1856. The combination of poor land, small holdings and outdated farming practices meant that Kiltubrid was still an impoverished rural parish at the end of the 19th century.

3. People

In this chapter we will look at population patterns in the parish of Kiltubrid, especially the emigration and seasonal migration during the second half of the 19th century. We will also look at communities, families and individuals within the parish in the 1890s and consider some of their characteristics and habits.

The parish of Kiltubrid was declared a 'congested district' under the terms of the land act of 1891, though Arthur Balfour was at pains to point out that such districts were 'not congested in the sense of being crowded, but congested by not being able to draw from their holdings a sufficient livelihood for themselves and their children'.[1] So Kiltubrid was congested not due to the density of its population but rather because of the impoverished condition of the people there. However this inland parish was not as poor as some of the 'really congested' districts along the western seaboard.[2] In the year 1891 there were 3,432 people living in the parish giving a density of one person per 3.5 statute acres which is not very densely populated even taking into consideration the fact that almost one quarter of the land in Kiltubrid consisted of mountain, woodland, bog or lake.[3]

Kiltubrid had been more congested in 1841 when there were 7,228 people living in the parish.[4] The Catholic parish records reflect this large population in several different ways. In the month of January 1841 there were 21 baptisms in St Brigid's Church, Drumcong, and in the first two months of that year there were 19 marriages recorded in the parish, with six weddings on one day, 22 February 1841.[5] The Famine took its toll on the people and the population of the parish had dropped by 27 per cent to 5,287 in 1851.[6] The decrease in population varied greatly from townland to townland within the parish with some townlands actually gaining in numbers while other dropped dramatically.[7]

The townland of Gortnawan, situated high on Slieve an Iarainn mountain, had a population of 198 in 1841 and 73 in 1851, a drop of 58 per cent. The townland of Drumparsons fared even worse dropping from a population of 46 in 1841 to just one in 1851 – a drop of 97.8 per cent. The village of Keshcarrigan lost only 11.4 per cent of its population while the townland of Aghacashlaun actually increased its population by 14.5 per cent during the Famine decade.[8]

A pattern of high emigration from the parish was established during the Famine and continued, though at a decreased rate, between the years 1851 and 1901.[9] The population of the parish dropped sharply during the Famine

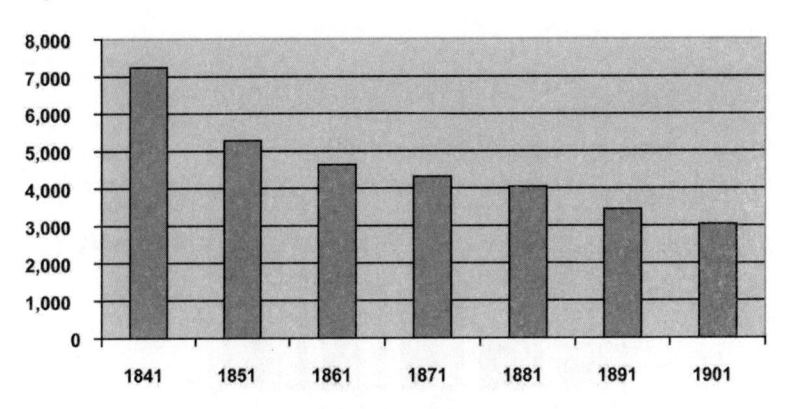

4.1 The population of Kiltubrid at ten-year intervals between 1841 and 1901

and again between the years 1871 and 1881, due largely to the economic depression that hit the country between 1877 and 1879. A combination of cheap American imports and a consequent fall in agricultural prices, a series of bad harvests culminating in the very wet summer of 1879,[10] and a fall off in demand for migratory labour,[11] meant that there was little option for many but to emigrate (fig. 4.2).

Emigration from Co. Leitrim varied from year to year in the decades after the Famine. It peaked immediately after the Famine and again in the period 1880 to 1883 due to the depressed agricultural economy of that time. In the first years after the Famine more females than males emigrated from the county. Later the situation was reversed with more males emigrating than females.[12]

There had been some emigration from the parish in the pre-Famine years though the number leaving was relatively small. In the year 1836 the parish priest of Kiltubrid, John Maguire, reported that between 20 and 30 individuals had emigrated from the parish in the previous three years and that they had gone 'chiefly to Canada'.[13]

The situation changed dramatically after the Great Famine with much greater numbers emigrating. Their destinations were more varied too, but in general they went to the east coast of the United States of America and to cities in the north of England and in Scotland. Three people born in Kiltubrid within three weeks of each other in the month of December 1881 suggest this pattern. Maria Duignan, who was born on 9 December 1881 in the townland of Drumruekill, emigrated and married Michael Rourke in Boston in 1912. Charles Redihan, from the townland of Letterfine, was born on 26 December 1881. He emigrated and married Rose O'Neill in Providence, New Jersey, in 1910. Francis Early, born on 31 December 1881 in Corderry Moreton, emigrated and married Helena O'Brien in Edinburgh in 1908.[14]

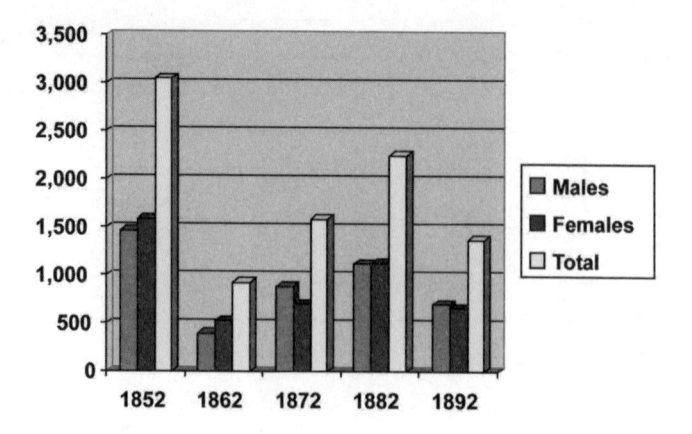

4.2 The number of people who emigrated from Co. Leitrim at ten-year intervals from 1852 to 1892

The pattern of emigration from the parish, triggered off largely by the Great Famine, was well established by the 1890s. Henry Doran's report to the Congested Districts Board, dated 31 January 1895, stated that:

> A large proportion of the young people (male and female) reared in this district emigrate to America before they reach twenty-five years of age.[15]

The seasonal migration of men from the west of Ireland to work at the harvesting of crops in the north of England and in Scotland was already a reality before the Great Famine.[16] This pattern continued after the Famine and even though Leitrim had the lowest rate of seasonal migration in Connacht it had the sixth highest rate of any county in Ireland (table 4.1). In the year

Table 4.1 Counties with the highest rate of seasonal migration in Ireland, 1891

Mayo	33.3	per 1,000
Roscommon	12.2	per 1,000
Sligo	7.6	per 1,000
Donegal	7.1	per 1,000
Galway	6.4	per 1,000
Leitrim	3.8	per 1,000

Source: Agricultural statistics, Ireland 1891, reports and tables relating to migratory agricultural labourers, HC (1891), xci, p.526.

1880, when the agricultural economy was still depressed, 1,289 people left Co. Leitrim to work as seasonal labourers. In that year Leitrim had the fourth highest rate of seasonal migration in Ireland with an estimated 4.1 per cent of all males in the county over the age of 20 being seasonal workers.[17] The number had dropped to 958 in 1881 and 740 in 1882.[18] In 1891 a total of 13,129 seasonal migrants left Ireland, with 84.3 per cent of these coming from the province of Connacht.[19] Only 294 of these came from Co. Leitrim, the county with the smallest number of seasonal migrants in Connacht.

Seasonal migration to the north of England and Scotland and emigration to England and America were essential for the economic survival of families in Kiltubrid in the 1890s (table 3.2). Henry Doran, in his report to the Congested Districts Board, stated that:

> The majority of those [from Kiltubrid] who migrate to England and Scotland leave home between April and June, and return in November. Their average earnings there vary a great deal, ranging from 15s to 25s per week. They save and send or bring home, from £8 to £10 per man on average.[20]

Permanent emigration and even the more temporary seasonal migration meant that there were many painful partings for the people of Kiltubrid in the 1890s. However, there was little choice in the matter. There was not a living for all of them at home.

One of the disadvantages of taking a parish as a geographical unit for the study of local history is that it may not be a natural community at all. Certain questions need to be asked: Was Kiltubrid a single community in the 1890s? What was the world view of the people of Kiltubrid at this time?

When J. Chambers, the school inspector, visited Keshcarrigan National School on 21 February 1895 he reported that the 'third class had little or no acquaintance with the map of the world.'[21] One month earlier Henry Doran stated that a mountainous area between Kiltubrid and Ballinaglera was known locally as 'Spike' because it was deemed to be as inaccessible as the 'convict station of Spike Island.'[22] Two years earlier Leland L. Duncan wrote that 'until the Cavan, Leitrim & Roscommon Light Railway was constructed a few years ago [in 1887] Kiltubrid was quite cut off from outside influence.'[23] To these outsiders the people of Kiltubrid must have appeared insular and myopic in their outlook. Yet, we must remember that America, England and Scotland were as real to the people of Kiltubrid as the neighbouring counties were because of the high rate of emigration and seasonal migration from the parish to the last two of these destinations. The reality was that many people lived their lives in small pockets or communities never moving far from where they were born. They lived their lives largely isolated from the bigger world.

The marriage patterns of the people of Kiltubrid in the 1890s – particularly where they choose their partner from – give a good insight into the communities that existed there at that time. On 18 February 1895 James Bohan from Gortnagullion married Anna McWeeney from the same townland. This was not unusual. Of the 136 marriages recorded in the 1890s in the Roman Catholic marriage register for Kiltubrid, 9.6 per cent of the weddings were couples where both partners came from the same townland. On 26 January 1899 Anna Gilmore from Aghacashlaun married John Ward from the neighbouring townland of Drumhubrid. A total of 17.6 per cent of the weddings in the parish in the 1890s were similar with the partners coming from adjoining townlands. Almost 80 per cent of the marriages that took place in St Brigid's Church, Drumcong in the 1890s were of couples where both partners came from within the parish or where one of the partners came from an adjacent townland in a neighbouring parish. In general people tended to marry someone who lived nearby or someone who lived within a radius of three miles from their birthplace. Parish boundaries were irrelevant in this process of selecting a partner.

There were three main marrying communities in the parish at this time (fig. 4.3). People from the northern end of the parish tended to marry someone from within that area or from the nearby townlands in the adjacent parishes of Drumshanbo, Ballinaglera and Aughnasheelin. (See section marked 'A' in figure 4.3) A total of 28.7 per cent of all the couples married in St Brigid's Church in the 1890s were from this area. A further 24.3 per cent of the couples came from the middle section of the parish, marked 'B' in figure 4.3, which included Annadale, Drumcong and Kilclare and townlands in the neighbouring parishes of Fenagh and Kiltoghert. A total of 21.3 per cent of the couples came from the Keshcarrigan area of the parish or from townlands bordering Kiltubrid in the neighbouring parishes of Fenagh and Mohill. This is the area marked 'C' in figure 4.3. People tended to marry within pockets or communities. People from section A did not marry people from section C and generally people from section B did not marry people from sections A or C. If we divide the parish into these three separate areas or marriage communities it accounts for 74.3 per cent of all the weddings which took place in Kiltubrid in the 1890s. The marriage records for the parish of Kiltubrid in the 1890s would suggest that there were at least three separate communities in the parish at that time.

The Gaelic football clubs which were set up in the parish between 1889 and 1892 further emphasize the divisions that existed between the communities in the parish in late Victorian times. Although the Gaelic Athletic Association was founded in 1884, it was not until five years later, early in 1889, that there was any attempt to organize a branch of that association in Kiltubrid. On Sunday 21 April 1889 a group of people met and founded the 'The Kiltubrid Michael Davitt' club.[24] The title of the club was carefully

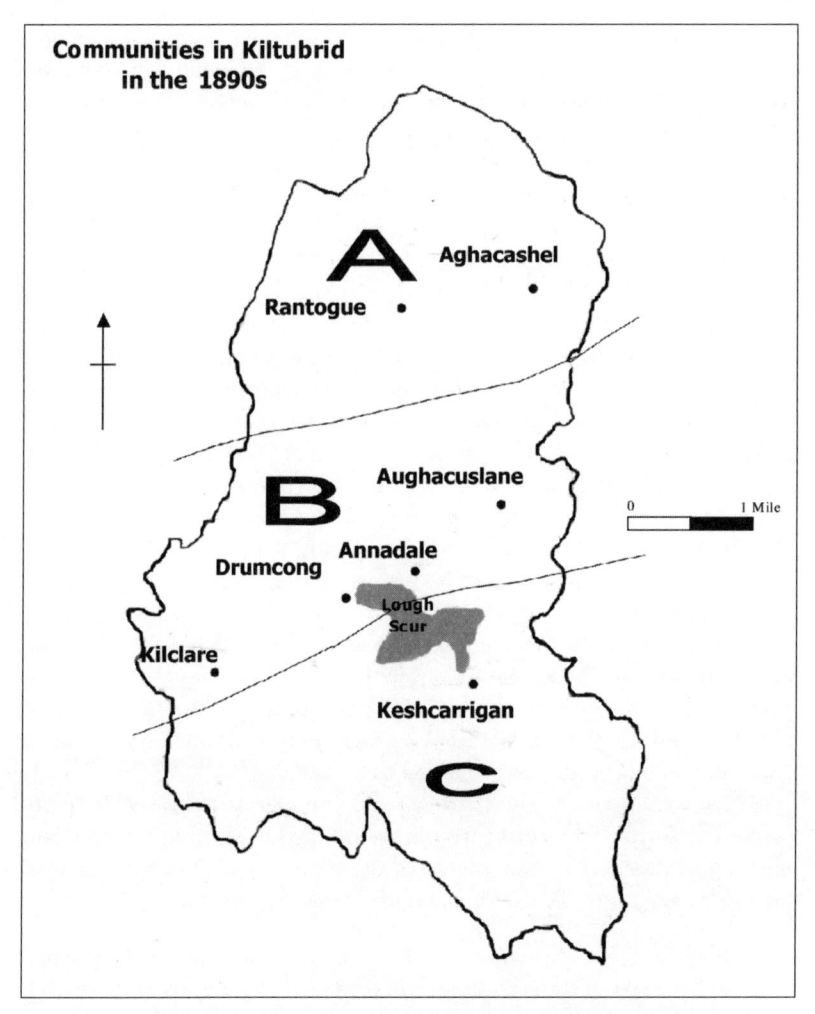

4.3 Map of Kiltubrid showing marriage patterns in the 1890s

chosen to represent the views of its members and their first match was played on 31 May 1889 [Ascension Day] 'on the grounds of an evicted farm outside the town [of Drumshanbo]'.[25] The club began with great fanfare and over one hundred members attended their early practices.[26] The name of the new club would suggest that it was a parish team. However, the officers, members and players of this club were from the Kilclare, Drumcong and Annadale areas of the parish and were not representative of the whole parish. This is the area of the parish marked 'B' in figure 4.3.

At the Leitrim County Convention of the Gaelic Athletic Association, held in Drumshanbo on 24 October 1889, an attempt was made by James

Rutledge and Bernard Bohan from the Keshcarrigan area to have a second GAA club, called 'Keshcarrigan Sullivans' set up in the parish. This area corresponds to the section of the parish represented by section 'C' in figure 4.3. The Convention was not in favour of this development. It felt that having two clubs in one parish would weaken the Irish National League there and it persuaded all the delegates from Kiltubrid to meet, sort out their differences and to try to set up one strong club in the parish which would be called 'Kiltubrid William Redmonds.'[27]

The new club was set up though it only survived for a few months and during that time it was torn apart by squabbles between the members from different areas of the parish. The president of the newly formed 'Kiltubrid William Redmonds', Peter Maguire from Derrien, tried his best to bring unity to the club and he even took the drastic step of having a notice placed in the *Roscommon Herald* asserting that 'there is no Gaelic club affiliated in this parish of Kiltubride [*sic*] only the one known as the Redmond club.'[28] His efforts were in vain. The Redmonds club disintegrated and by March 1890 there were two affiliated clubs in the parish, 'Kiltubrid Michael Davitts' and the 'Keshcarrigan Sullivans' the former coming from section 'B' of the parish and the latter coming from section 'C.' Both clubs were preparing to compete against each other in the first ever county championship to be played in Leitrim. The County Convention of the GAA had to accept the reality that there was more than one community within the parish of Kiltubrid and it was obvious that there were deep divisions between these communities that could not be glossed over easily.

There were divisions elsewhere as well. The split in the Parnellite party percolated down to this rural parish in the north west of Ireland. A turbulent meeting of the County Committee of the GAA was held in Keshcarrigan on 8 February 1891. The chairman pleaded with the meeting saying:

> I believe that in the course of a few days the differences that has arisen in the ranks of the Irish Party will be settled and it is our duty to keep silent as to such time as they do. For myself I am in favour of Mr Parnell but for peace sake I would rather keep silent at present because it does not matter a pin what we do in this matter. It will be abler men that will settle this affair.'[29]

But his pleading fell on deaf ears. The meeting split and voted by a majority of one against Parnell. The two delegates from Kiltubrid who were present at the meeting abstained.

During the year 1891 football matches in the county were disrupted by disputes between those who backed Parnell and those who opposed him. The 'Keshcarrigan Sullivans' club was, it appears, mostly anti-Parnellite and the *Roscommon Herald* reported that after they had played a match on St Patrick's Day 1891

... hundreds of fine young men of the parish marched up and down the streets [of Keshcarrigan] cheering for Justin McCarthy and groans for Parnell. This manifestation of true nationality the police could not bear, but the young men had their way and all returned home well pleased.'[30]

The differences between the two Kiltubrid GAA clubs were obvious and their disputes acrimonious. They were due to play each other in the championship of 1891. The 'Kiltubrid Michael Davitt club had, it appears, pro-Parnellite players in its ranks and the 'Keshcarrigan Sullivans' objected to playing them on the grounds that they had players from Drumshanbo 'where rowdyism exists.'[31] A branch of the 'Irish National Federation', which seceded from the 'Irish National League' because of its anti-Parnellite stance, was set up in the parish in the Autumn of 1891. The curate, John Quinn, was elected president of the branch.[32] This development did not succeed in unifying the parish. By the spring of 1892 the GAA in the county and in Kiltubrid was hopelessly divided on the Parnellite issue and at a meeting of the County Committee of the GAA which was held in Keshcarrigan in February 1892 it was resolved that:

> No championship be played off this year in Leitrim, not on account of the difference in the Irish ranks, for we the Gaels of Leitrim are all marching under the branch of the Federation, and by having no championship it will leave us better cemented as Irishmen and as Gaels.[33]

There was virtually no GAA activity in Kiltubrid or in Leitrim from 1892 until 1904 because of the deep divisions caused by the Parnellite split. When a new club was formed in Kiltubrid in 1904 it was, rather pointedly and optimistically, called 'Kiltubrid United Gaels.'[34]

The GAA activity and divisions in Kiltubrid between 1889 and 1892 spell out more clearly than anything else the fact that there was more than one community in the parish at that time. The divisions in the GAA ranks were mainly between the sections of the parish marked B and C in figure 4.3.[35] The Rantogue and Aughacashel area to the north of the parish, that is section A, was not involved in these divisions merely because it appears to have had little interest in Gaelic football. The separateness of this northern section of the parish was further emphasized in 1909 with the building of St Joseph's mountain chapel at Rantogue.[36] The divisions, suggested by the marriage patterns in the 1890s, are spelled out more clearly by the very public divisions within the ranks of the GAA at this time. These local divisions preceded the divisions in the Parnellite party. The Parnellite crisis merely added fuel to the fire.

So the parish of Kiltubrid cannot be called a community at this time. It was made up of three or perhaps even more small communities. St Brigid's Church, Drumcong, was the only Catholic church in the parish at this time.[37]

This church and the strong presence of the parish priests Hugh Brennan (1880–96) and Anthony McGaver (1896–1933) was a unifying force in the parish. However the landscape of the parish, with Lough Scur and the Ballinamore/Ballyconnell canal right in the middle of it, worked against parish unity. There were ten primary schools in the parish in 1891 and this too created division rather than unity. Henry Doran noted in 1895 that the absence of roads and bridges and the poor quality of the roads militated against travel in the parish.[38]

The opening of the Cavan & Leitrim Railway in 1887 helped for those who wished to travel to Ballinamore or Drumshanbo and could afford the fare.[39] Horses were scarce and consequently few people travelled on horseback or in carts or coaches. Leland L. Duncan noted in his diary on 12 August 1892 that Willie Peyton came from Driney to Annadale 'on his bicycle.' Cycling clubs were being set up in Ireland, especially along the east coast, at this time and cycling was becoming popular and fashionable among the better off people. J.C. Perry, the editor of the *Irish Wheelman*, wrote in the issue of 9 November 1897, that:

> Cycling has now finally found its level [in Ireland], which happily is a very high one. It is no longer a fad or a fancy, but an established factor in modern everyday life.[40]

He was a cycling enthusiast and in his eagerness to promote the sport was given to exaggeration. However, bicycles were a rarity in Leitrim at this time. Willie Peyton, who lived in Driney House, had a bicycle. He came from a small landed gentry family and could afford it. Most could not afford a bicycle which ranged in price from £8 to £20 in this period.[41] Mr Perry was being very optimistic. It was not until the 1930s that bicycles became common place in Leitrim and people could travel greater distances with relative ease.[42]

The landscape, mountain, lakes, rivers, canal, roads and bridges were all factors in determining the communities at this period. So too were the National Schools and the small halls where the people socialized. If people wished to travel in the 1890s they had, in most instances, to walk. Travel was slow and arduous and the majority of those who did not emigrate or migrate from the parish socialized and lived their lives within a few mile radius of where they were born. The exception was their visit to the fairs and markets in the local towns. Kiltubrid could not, by any stretch of the imagination, be called a community at this time. It was made up of at least three separate communities which paid little respect to parish boundaries.

A quantitative and statistical approach to history is necessary when dealing with population trends. However, a purely statistical approach seems to reduce human beings to numbers and fails to capture their individuality

4.4 The McManus family, 15 August 1892

or their personality. Studying families and individuals can help counteract this. In the previous section we looked at the communities in the parish in the 1890s. Here we look at families, the most basic community of all. In particular we look at two families, the McManus family from Aughrim and the Slacke family from Annadale. These two families lived within a mile of one another. Both families were photographed by Leland L. Duncan though they had little else in common. The Slacke family belonged to the landlord class and the McManus family were tenant farmers.

The McManus family from the townland of Aughrim is a fairly typical family from this period and this place (fig. 4.4). This photograph, taken in 1892, shows Patrick McManus (51), his wife Mary (51) and their two youngest children, Michael (12) and Jane (11). We know from the Catholic parish records that Patrick and Mary McManus had six other children born between 1862 and 1877 who, most likely, had emigrated like many of their contemporaries.[43] We learn from Griffith's Valuation that the McManus family had a house and 15 acres of land with a rateable valuation of £6 15s. We know from Leland Duncan's unpublished diary that the McManus household was one where people visited and where there was a fund of stories and folktales. Michael had inherited many of these folktales from his mother and grandfather, and when he was fourteen he wrote some of them down for Duncan who later had them published in the London quarterly called *Folk-Lore*.[44] We know from that same diary that Michael McManus almost cut off his finger with a scythe on 18 August 1892.

All this information helps to flesh out the McManus family and removes them from the realms of numbers and statistics. However, nothing can quite achieve this in the way a photograph can. This photograph gives human faces and bodies to these people. We can now see them in a new way that words or figures, no matter how detailed, could never achieve.

Knowing when a photograph was taken is of vital importance for the purpose of research. We are lucky in this instance because we know that Leland L. Duncan took this photograph on Monday 15 August 1892.[45] This is obviously a posed photograph with the photographer choosing his angle carefully and getting the family to focus on a point to his left. This is an excellent example of late Victorian photography and the family being dressed so well can be explained by the fact that the photograph was taken on the feast of the Assumption after they had returned from Mass.[46]

Four other photographs of Michael McManus, taken by Duncan, have survived. In three of them he is dressed in rough working clothes, hob-nailed boots, dark trousers and waist coat, a long sleeved white shirt buttoned tightly to his neck and a cap jauntily sitting on his head. The more photographs one has relating to the same person or place the better from the historian's point of view. So the photograph of the McManus family, the several photographs of Michael McManus, the photograph of the McManus house in fig. 2.1 and the photograph of the hearth inside the house,[47] all of which were taken between 1889 and 1894, are invaluable primary sources for the study of this family and the world they inhabited. When taken along with the other historical sources relating to them we can build up a comprehensive picture of the McManus family.

The Slacke family which lived at Annadale House was one of the few landed gentry families in the parish (fig. 4.5). Theirs was a small estate, never bigger than five hundred acres. James Wilkinson Slacke, the head of the household in the 1890s, was not a landlord in the usual sense of that word since he worked as a solicitor and represented people at the local district courts in Ballinamore, Mohill and Carrick on Shannon. The Slackes had come to Ireland from Slacke Hall in Derbyshire in the late 17th century, settled on the old monastic site of Cill Tiobraid and set up ironworks in the county.[48] When William Slacke married his first cousin, Angel Anna Slacke, in 1764 he had the house renamed 'Annadale' in her honour. Later Angel Anna Slacke became a Methodist and Annadale House became a meeting place for the local Methodist society and a place where the weary preachers could rest. John Wesley stayed there in May 1787 and again in May 1789.[49] Methodism was on the wane in the parish during the first decades of the 19th century and by the year 1891 there were only seven Methodists living in the parish, most of whom had been born outside the county.[50]

Kiltubrid was predominantly Roman Catholic, though several of the tenants on the Slacke estate were members of the Church of Ireland. There

People

4.5 The Slacke family at Annadale House, August 1889

were virtually no Presbyterians in the parish. Of the 3,474 people living in the parish in 1891 a total of 96.9 per cent were Roman Catholic and 2.8 per cent were Church of Ireland.

In 1890 James Wilkinson Slacke married his first cousin Caroline Annette Duncan, a sister of the photographer Leland L. Duncan. After the marriage she left her home in London and went to live at Annadale. James Wilkinson Slacke was a keen sportsman and despite losing his right arm in a shooting accident he continued as a member of the North Shannon Yacht Club and the County Leitrim Gun Club.[51] His mother, Susan Slacke, his wife Carrie and his sisters Harriette and Ethel were involved in local Church of Ireland charitable activities.[52]

Duncan's photograph of the family, taken at the hall door of Annadale House in August 1889 is a fine photograph cleverly constructed. He used the archway surrounding the main doorway of the house to frame the picture. The grandeur of the doorway and the finery in which the family is dressed is in stark contrast to some of the other photographs Duncan took of other people and houses in the area. Photographs capture this contrast better than the written word.

James Wilkinson Slacke died as a result of a freak accident in January 1908, while staying in the Bush Hotel, Carrick on Shannon, during the Quarter Sessions there. He tripped on the stairs, and having no right hand to grab the banister, he fell to the ground and died a few days later as a result of the injuries

4.6 Mrs Mary Ward, 1892

he sustained.[53] Shortly after his death the Slacke family left Annadale, going first to Dublin before settling in Rhosneigr in the Isle of Anglesey.[54] The Slacke family was the last of the landlord families to leave Kiltubrid.

In this section we will look at two individuals, Mary Ward, a housewife and mother from the townland of Drumadkey and Mikey Lynch, a bachelor and farm worker on the Annadale estate who lived in the townland of Leitrim. The photograph shown in fig. 4.6 would, at first sight, appear to capture the late Victorian period and be a rich source of information for the historian. However, it is not as useful as it appears to be. This photograph raises several questions: Did Duncan take a photograph of the spinning wheel because it was typical or because it was unusual? Was the spinning work done outdoors, or did Duncan merely ask for the spinning wheel to be taken outdoors to ensure better light for the picture? Is Mrs Ward's dressed in her everyday clothes or did she dress up for the photograph? Are the clothes she is wearing typical of the clothes worn by other women in Leitrim at this time?[55]

This photograph of Mary Ward seems to raise more questions than it gives answers. Yet there is much that the historian can glean from it. Her

4.7 Mikey Lynch, 1889

ankle-length black dress, her black shawl and white bonnet all match the severity of the expression on her face.[56] The neatness of the woman's dress, the spinning wheel – despite its makeshift leg – the whitewashed wall of the house, the latticed window opened to ventilate the house with the August air and the creeper plant growing on the wall all suggest a relative degree of comfort and prosperity.[57] Yet we cannot draw general conclusions about dress or the prevalence of spinning wheels[58] in the area from this particular photograph. Several other photographs that Duncan took of this family have survived.[59]

Mikey Lynch, a farm labourer on the Annadale estate, lived in the townland of Leitrim with his brother Johnny and his sister Winnie. They had no land[60] and both brothers worked away from home, Johnny as a plasterer and Mikey as a farm labourer.[61] There are no baptismal records for Mikey Lynch nor are there any marriage records because he, like his brother and sister, did not marry.[62] Because of this scarcity of records relating to him the photographs Leland L. Duncan took of him take on a greater importance (fig. 4.7).

The photograph in fig. 4.7 is an excellent, full-length photograph of Mikey Lynch wearing his working clothes and framed by two gaunt trees in the background. His clothes are the typical working clothes of the time – a long sleeved shirt tightly buttoned at the wrists and neck, boots, trousers, waistcoat and hat which he has taken off in order to pose for the photograph. He obviously is in some discomfort because his left hand is curled into a fist. Having an Englishman, with a strange accent and an even stranger contraption called a camera, take your photograph could be quite an ordeal for someone unused to it. Three years later the people were more comfortable with Duncan taking their photographs. Sunday 21 August 1892 was 'a fair day, rather cloudy but no rain' Duncan wrote in his diary so he made good use of the suitable weather to take photographs of 'lots of groups.'[63] Having taken the pictures he stated that 'The people [were] much pleased.' Part of the reason they were 'much pleased' was that he gave a total of 7s. 6d. to the people he photographed that day.[64]

Three other photographs of Mikey Lynch have survived. Two of them are good quality photographs. One of them shows him trimming the evergreen trees at Annadale with a sickle or 'hook' as it was known locally.[65] A homemade wooden ladder, with uneven spacing between the steps, enabled him to trim the trees higher up. In this photograph, taken in August 1892, he is wearing a short jacket over his waistcoat, his hat is on his head and, significantly, his left hand is no longer in a fist. He had, in the three years since 1889, become accustomed to the camera and the photographer.

The photograph of Mikey with his brother Johnny and sister Winnie at home in the summer of 1893 is one of Duncan's best photographs.[66] In this photograph Mikey is dressed up for the occasion with hat and jacket, though without any fancy cravat or necktie, like those worn by some of the other men in the area when they were dressed in their Sunday best clothes. The close-up photograph allows us to see Mikey's long hoary locks and his brother Johnny's full beard. Johnny is dressed somewhat better than Mikey with jacket, waistcoat cravat and neatly fitting cap.[67] Winnie has a large shawl wrapped around her and loose wisps of hair hanging around her head. She is not dressed as well as most of the other women photographed by Duncan, though she has a wonderful expression on her face – a desire to please and the faint suggestion of a smile. The fourth surviving photograph of Mikey Lynch has him working as part of a meitheal building a rick of hay.[68] He obviously moved his head during the exposure as his features are rather blurred. In this photograph he is pictured in his shirt sleeves, with braces showing. However, despite the warm nature of the work, he has the shirt buttoned tightly at the neck and wrists and his hat on his head.[69]

It is easy to describe what Mikey Lynch looks like in these photographs, but it is a more difficult and risky process trying to deduce from them what type of personality he had, what his mental outlook was. In these photographs, even the later ones, he appears to be diffident and lacking in confidence. Francis Mulvanerty, on the other hand, who was also a farm worker on the Annadale estate, is pictured with a broad confident smile, and while his working clothes are very similar to those of Mikey Lynch, his best clothes are much superior.[70] We learn much more about Mikey Lynch's interior world from the folklore Leland L. Duncan gathered from him than we do from the photographs. His stories about 'the good people' are very similar to those collected by Douglas Hyde and others at this period, though Mikey Lynch's stories have been grounded very much in the local area. Mikey Lynch related this story to Duncan:

> The flat bottom known as Beirne's rock on the northern side of Leitrim townland, Kiltubrid parish, used in the olden time to be a favourite place of resort for the good people, and great fights used to take place there, the parties fighting all the way up the lonesome valley which lies between the townlands of Lisdrumacrone and Corglass. On Lisdrumacrone there was a house, now pulled down, where lived a widow woman and her young children. One night there was a great fight all up the hill between the two bands of fairies, and the house coming in their way, they burst in at the back door and out of the front, fighting through the house. The woman was naturally greatly alarmed, and ran at once up to the room to see were her children safe. She found them quietly asleep, and in the morning all the doors were shut again. Some of the people say that she found a head under the bed, and that was the only evidence of the fight to be seen.[71]

The fact that Mikey Lynch knew these folktales and probably believed in them gives us an insight into his interior world. He was, we can conclude, superstitious though he was not exceptional in this. Duncan was able to gather folktales from Barney, Francis and Anne Whelan,[72] Michael and Mary McManus, Ellen Egan,[73] and Edward McVittie,[74] all of whom lived within one mile of Annadale House.[75] Folktales, superstitions and beliefs in spirits were widespread, not just in Kiltubrid, but throughout much of rural Ireland in the 1890s. It was at this time, in the month of March 1895, that Bridget Cleary was killed in Co. Tipperary because it was believed that she was possessed by fairies or evil spirits.[76] One year later, in March 1896, in a less well known case, James Cunningham was killed at Lisphelan in Co. Roscommon. His killing, like that of Bridget Cleary, took place in a haze of ignorance, superstition and fear.[77] Mikey Lynch was not exceptionally superstitious. He was merely a man of his time.

Clothes styles are always changing. They are an extension of the person and can give insights into the one who wears them. In this section we will take a brief look at the type of clothes the people of Kiltubrid were wearing in the 1890s and how these had evolved from the beginning of the 19th century.

Most accounts of the way people were dressed in Leitrim in the 19th century describe poverty, wretchedness and rags. James McParlan's account of the way the men were dressed, written in 1802, was an exception:

> The clothing is remarkably neat, clean and strong. The coat is most commonly of frize [sic], which is made up for about 20s. – the breeches always corderoy, and some fancy waistcoat, are made up for about 20s. more; the hat shoes, shirt and stockings come to 16s.[78]

The women and children were dressed much more shabbily. General Jean Sarrazin, one of the generals in Humbert's French force which arrived in north Connacht on 22 August 1798 and passed through Kiltubrid on 7 September, was shocked by the poverty he encountered. He wrote:

> We were astonished by the extreme poverty which appeared everywhere before our eyes, right from the beginning of our encounters with Ireland. Never has any country presented such an unhappy perspective, the women and children are practically naked.[79]

Edward Wakefield's account, 12 years later, stated that:

> The poor throughout Connaught live in a state of great wretchedness ... The clothing of the men consists of frieze, that of the women of linsey, both manufactured by themselves, and dyed a dark snuff colour, with oak sawdust, which has a most gloomy appearance.[80]

A similar picture emerges in 1836 when the labouring classes of Co. Leitrim were said to be dressed miserably. It was reported from the barony of Dromahair that:

> There is a great deal of nakedness, partly through sloth and partly through necessity. A man has, perhaps, one good suit, which he wears on the fifty two Sundays of the year and on a few holidays, but all the rest of the time he is in rags ... It is rare to see a man without shoes, not so as to the women, and still less so as to the children; the use however of shoes and stockings is increasing. The only portion of their clothing which the women are accustomed to make is their shifts.[81]

A priest from the barony of Mohill stated that 'I have known people to come to first Mass in decent clothes, and when it was over, run home and exchange with others, to enable them to appear at late prayers.'[82] From the same barony it was reported that the:

> Children everywhere were scarcely protected from the weather, especially the boys, who were often without trowsers, and sometimes removed but by a shirt from a state of even indecent nudity.[83]

Throughout the 19th century the tenant farmers and cottiers of Leitrim and their families were, by and large, dressed miserably. The men were best dressed, though their working clothes were often mere rags. Women were shabbily and children scantily dressed and these were the ones most likely to be found barefooted. By 1836 homemade frieze and linen were being replaced in Leitrim by English clothes which could be produced much cheaper.[84] By the 1890s most of the people of Kiltubrid were buying these clothes. Henry Doran explained that:

> A large number of poorer people get their outer clothing from pedlars who take van loads of second-hand clothing to the weekly markets and dispose of them there by a form of auction peculiar to the trade.[85]

The photographs of Leland L. Duncan are the best primary source for studying the dress of the people of Kiltubrid in the late 19th century. Laura Jones, in her article 'Photography and ethnological research'[86] warns the researcher 'of the need for caution in drawing conclusions on the basis of photographic evidence alone'.[87] It is true that the researcher must place photographic evidence alongside other primary sources whenever possible and test the information contained in them in this way. A single photograph, no matter how good it is, is of limited value to the historian and one must be careful about drawing conclusions from it. However, when there is a critical mass of photographs from a particular area and time then the photographic evidence, in itself, can be quite compelling. Leland L. Duncan took over one hundred photographs of people from the Kiltubrid area of Co. Leitrim between the years 1889 and 1894. He photographed them in many different situations and on different days of the week. This body of photographic evidence built up by Duncan allows us to confidently draw certain conclusions about the way people dressed in this place and time. Photographs, paintings and sketches can capture the dress styles of a period in a way that the written word cannot do.

Based on the evidence of Duncan's photographs we can conclude that in general the men of Kiltubrid were dressed well on Sundays and holydays. They wore, on these days, a rough tweed suit, waistcoat, shirt with high collar and cravat or large necktie. They were less well dressed on weekdays when they dressed in hob-nailed boots, rough trousers, sometimes patched or torn, and braces, a long-sleeved collar-less shirt buttoned tightly at the neck and wrists, a waistcoat and hat or cap. When the weather was cooler they wore a short jacket coat over the waistcoat. Most of the men sported hair on their faces, a full beard, long locks or moustache.

The women generally were dressed in a dark or black ankle-length dress, with a dark shawl draped over their shoulders. They wore bonnets or head-scarves rather than hats. They wore their hair parted in the centre and tied back tightly into a bun at the back of their heads. Most of the women wore aprons when at home.[88] Three of the women Duncan photographed were barefooted.

The young women dressed differently. They did not wear bonnets, scarves or shawls and they generally wore their hair tied up on top of their heads. One young woman, 'Fair'[89] Ellen Ward, from the townland of Drumadkey and a daughter of the woman with the spinning wheel, was photographed twice by Duncan.[90] She was wearing a different dress on each occasion. Both dresses were long ankle-length ones with tight waists, wide belts and high collars. One dress was dark coloured the other being bright coloured with a floral design. Her dress, unlike that of some of the older women, is in the late Victorian fashion and compares favourably with that of her much wealthier neighbour, Harriette Slacke from Annadale House.[91] Ellen Ward's dresses may have come from America or it may be that the Wards, having a spinning wheel, a neat house (fig. 4.6) and 18.5 acres of land[92] could afford better and more fashionable clothes than their neighbours.[93] Another young woman, Brigid Whelan from the townland of Driney, is also dressed exceptionally well in a long bright dress of similar style to the ones worn by Ellen Ward.[94] Both women had their hair in tresses and neatly tied up on top of their heads. What is obvious is that there was a great difference in the way the younger and older women dressed.

The children were more likely to be barefooted than the women, though we must remember that Duncan took all of his photographs in the summer months when people were most likely to go barefooted. The children were, in general, well dressed. The boys under the age of five were as likely to be found wearing a dress as they were to be found wearing trousers. The boys of school-going age were dressed in short trousers which were narrow-legged and went to just below the knee. The boys and girls with footwear usually wore high-laced boots.

There was considerable variation in the quality and type of clothes worn. Much depended on whether the individual was a man, woman or child, on what age they were or on what day of the week it was. Some of the clothes were poor and ragged but generally they were quite good. However, we must be aware that those who were worst dressed probably shied away from having their photographs taken and that the people who had prior warning probably dressed up for the photographs.

Adelia Margery West, a cousin of the Slackes of Annadale, completed her memoirs in 1895. These memoirs, which are part of the Slacke family private papers, give a very good insight into the life of the landed class in Leitrim in the 19th century. She noted that her grandfather, 'Old Billy Slacke' was famous for having one of the most hospitable houses and the best food and wines in all of Leitrim at the beginning of the 1800s. She wrote:

The hours for meals in Leitrim were pretty much what they are now but under different names. Breakfast at nine, dinner at four, tea at six and supper at nine. Those who had a snack between breakfast and dinner had something like a glass of wine and a piece of cake ... My grandfather [William Slacke] was most particular about his tea which he choose himself ... and many a pound of both black and green tea was sent as a present to different friends when the Annadale chests were opened.[95]

Ned Murray, the steward at Annadale in the early 1800s, prepared the beef for the kitchen. Chicken and beef were regularly on the menu and when dinner was over 'on the cloth being removed the housekeeper [Mrs Riddell] came in and standing behind the master's chair drank the health of the family in a bumper of good old port.'[96] They had regular meals, plenty of food, a varied diet and rituals to go with it.

The diet of Leitrim's peasantry was very different at this time. The Defenders who rebelled in north Connacht in the period 1793–5 were concerned with practical issues such as the setting up of the militia, rents, tithes, dues and food. At a Defender meeting in May 1795 one speaker announced 'we have lived long enough on potatoes and salt, it is our turn now to eat beef and mutton.'[97] Fifty years later things had not changed very much. John Dukes, the medical doctor based in Mohill, reported in 1845 that the food of the lower classes

> is never better than potatoes and milk in summer, and in winter they do not have the milk. Sometimes they get a herring or stirabout [which] is considered wholesome food; but latterly they have not been able to get that.[98]

He went on to draw a distinction between the labourers who had no land and consequently no milk and the 'two-acre men' who had milk at certain times of the year. Another witness, the Revd George Gearty, parish priest of Annaduff, told the same inquiry that the potatoes people had were 'of the very worst description, they are not able to raise the better kind of potatoes and consequently they live upon lumpers.'[99] When the potato blight struck, famine inevitably followed.

The Great Famine of the mid 19th century had a big impact on Kiltubrid and affected it in many ways, most notably in the size of its population, the type of housing and the pattern of emigration and seasonal migration which followed. But other things such as the farming methods and diet of the people remained largely unchanged.

Henry Doran stated that in the 1890s the people of Kiltubrid had stirabout (made from Indian meal or oatmeal or a mixture of both) for breakfast between 1 April and 1 August each year. For the other half of the year they had potatoes and milk for breakfast, sometimes supplemented with a little bread and tea. Supper was the same as breakfast and, like breakfast, it varied depending on the availability of potatoes.[100]

Dinner also varied depending on the time of the year. From the 1 April to 1 August they had flour bread and tea and occasionally eggs for dinner. From 1 August to 1 April they had bread and tea or sometimes potatoes with cabbage seasoned with a small quantity of bacon fat. Salted herrings were also occasionally used with the potatoes.[101]

Potatoes, stirabout, milk and sometimes herrings was the staple diet of the people in pre-Famine Leitrim. The people of Kiltubrid still depended on these same foods for their nourishment in the 1890s. Little had changed in their diet, except that Indian meal was now available and they sometimes had cabbage and tea to supplement the other foods. There were no reports of starvation in the parish in the 1890s. This was due, not to changed farming methods or a changed diet, but rather to the fact that the land had to support less than half the population it had attempted to support in the years of the Great Famine. Besides virtually every household had money coming from family members who were working elsewhere, either temporarily or permanently.

Conclusion

Kiltubrid was a 'congested district', a euphemism for an impoverished parish, in the 1890s. The Famine had impacted greatly on the parish. The population had dropped by 27 per cent in the ten-year period between 1841 and 1851 and by 1901 it was just 41 per cent of what it had been 60 years earlier. The Famine triggered off a pattern of emigration that drained the parish of its young people. Seasonal migration, already established in the area before the Famine, continued after it. To survive in the 1890s many households needed to get one quarter of their yearly income from family members working outside the country.[1]

Some aspects of life in Kiltubrid had changed considerably during the 19th century and others aspects remained virtually unchanged. The greatest change in the lives of the people during the 1800s was the standard of their dwelling houses and outhouses. At the beginning of the 1800s the typical house in Leitrim was a small one-roomed thatched house that gave shelter to both animals and human beings. A total of 43.2 per cent of the houses in Leitrim were still one-roomed in 1841. These were the houses that were worst hit by the Famine and by 1901 only 1.8 per cent of the houses in Kiltubrid were one roomed. By then the three-roomed traditional thatched cottage was the norm with almost 80 per cent of the houses in the parish being of that type. These houses were used almost exclusively to give shelter to human beings because virtually every house with enough land to keep a cow had a cow-byre by then. These outhouses in the west of Ireland were small and thatched and were tiny in comparison to the outhouses to be found elsewhere in the country. The second half of the 19th century saw a dramatic improvement in both the dwelling houses and outhouses in the parish. The Famine had as big an impact on the built environment of Kiltubrid as it had on its demographic make-up.

The improvement in houses and outhouses in Kiltubrid during the 1800s would suggest increased prosperity during the course of the century and yet the reality is that the farming practices in Kiltubrid in the 1890s were much as they had been at the beginning of the 1800s. The loy spade was still their plough and the donkey, not the horse, their best pack animal. The land was still being exhausted without rotation of crops or proper fertilizing. The drainage problems that existed at the beginning of the century were still there at the end.

The fact that the agricultural practices had changed little from one end of the century to the other meant that the diet of the people had changed little too. Potatoes, milk, buttermilk, stirabout and sometimes herrings were the main elements of their diet in the decades before and after the Famine. There was less hunger in the 1890s merely because there were fewer mouths to feed. The people of Kiltubrid were, judging by the photographs of Leland L. Duncan, relatively well dressed in the 1890s and in this respect things had improved from the pre-Famine years. The snuff coloured home-made clothes of linsey and frieze of the early 1800s had, by the 1890s, given way to clothes bought second-hand at stalls in the local fairs and markets. While some of the women and children went barefooted in the 1890s there were none of the reports of the near nakedness or rags which were to be found in much of the west of Ireland in the early 1800s.

The photographs that Duncan took in Kiltubrid between the years 1889 and 1894 are among the most important primary historical sources for this study. Duncan's photographs, because of their quality and number, are an invaluable resource. He deliberately set out to document the society he visited in these years with his camera, pen and paper. I have used these photographs alongside other primary sources from the period to get an insight into the lives of the people who lived in this rural parish in the north west of Ireland in the 1890s.[2]

In the past historians used photographs at the publication stage of their work rather than at the research stage. They used them merely to embellish the written word, the already closed research. The historian who uses photographs, paintings, sketches, maps, the built environment, landscape, oral history and archaeology as well as the primary manuscript sources is approaching history in a rich multi-faceted way. Photographs must, when available, be part of the mix. They must be there from the beginning of the process and not just thrown in at the end, as an after-thought, to prettify.

Duncan photographed many groups of people – families, neighbours and meitheals. The picture one gets from the photographs, from marriage records and from the Gaelic football clubs in the parish is that people of Kiltubrid lived their lives in small pocket communities, seldom straying more than a few miles from home except to go to the markets in town, to travel for seasonal work or to emigrate permanently. It appears that there were at least three separate communities in Kiltubrid in the 1890s.

So we can conclude that the people who lived in Kiltubrid in the 1890s were relatively better off than their parents or grand-parents had been. The standard of living had improved from the pre-Famine years. And yet, despite some improvements during the course of the 19thcentury, Kiltubrid was in the 1890s, still a place struggling to survive, a parish 'on the verge of want'.

Notes

ABBREVIATIONS

GAA	Gaelic Athletic Association	NS	National School
HC	House of Commons	NUI	National University of Ireland
HL	House of Lords	PRO	Public Records Office (London)
HO	Home Office	RP	Rebellion papers
NAI	National Archives of Ireland	TCD	Trinity College Dublin
NLI	National Library of Ireland	UCD	University College Dublin

INTRODUCTION

1 I am indebted to Elizabeth Mans for giving me access to the Duncan photographs and to the private papers of the Slacke family.

1. HOUSES

1 For an account of the the rededication of the church see the *Leitrim Observer*, 27 Oct. 1891; Liam Kelly, *St Brigid's Church, Kiltubrid, County Leitrim, 1781–1995* (1995). 2 According to local tradition, the women of the parish paid for the bell from their egg money. 3 Liscarbin National School was built in 1884, Crummy in 1885, Keshcarrigan in 1890, Kilclare in 1894 and Aughacashel in 1904. 4 P.J. Flanagan, *The Cavan & Leitrim railway* (London, 1966); the Ballinamore – Ballyconnell Canal, was built as a famine relief works between 1846 and 1859. It too bisected the parish, but unlike the narrow gauge railway, it proved to be a white elephant until it was re-developed for leisure cruisers in the early 1990s. See P. Flanagan, *The Ballinamore & Ballyconnell Canal* (Devon, 1972) and idem, *The Shannon- Erne waterway* (Dublin, 1994). 5 Duncan took his Leitrim photographs during the summer months and when he returned to London he gave history talks mostly in the parish hall at Lewisham, and illustrated his talks with lantern slides of his photographs. 6 C. Ó Danachair, 'The questionnaire system' in *Béaloideas*, 15 (1945), pp 207–11; E. E. Evans, *The personality of Ireland* (3rd ed., Dublin, 1992), p. 54. Houses with a bed outshot were unusual in south Leitrim though one such house has survived in the Aghacashel area of the parish. See *An introduction to the architectural heritage of County Leitrim* (2004), p. 12. 7 NAI, Census of Ireland 1901. 8 For different types of sash windows see A. Gailey, *Rural houses of the north of Ireland* (Edinburgh, 1984), pp 134–9. 9 L. Kelly, *The face of time* (Dublin, 1995), p. 62. 10 Duncan's photograph of the house of Patrick Winters in the townland of Corglass bears out this point. See Kelly, *The face of time*, p. 43. 11 J. McParlan, *Statistical survey of the County Leitrim* (Dublin, 1802), pp 43–4. 12 Appendix (E) to first report of commissioners for inquiring into the condition of the poorer classes in Ireland, HC 1836, xxxii, p. 40. 13 Most traveller's accounts refer to the smoke-filled houses in the west of Ireland. A verse written in 1675 describes 'Their cabbins, full of Dirt and Smoak, Enough an English Man to Choake.' Cited in F.H.A. Aalen, 'The evolution of the traditional house in western Ireland' in *Journal of the Royal Society of Antiquaries of Ireland* 96 (1966), p. 56. 14 A. Young, *A tour in Ireland, 1776–1779* (2 vols; London, 1780), ii, pp 47–8. 15 G. Stokes (ed.), *Pococke's tour in Ireland in 1752* (Dublin, 1891), p. 63. The research of F.H.A. Aalen confirms that the majority of houses in the west of Ireland had two doors and not one. See 'The evolution of the traditional house' p. 49. 16 'Iter Hibernicum or the Ramble, being the voyage and adventure of Three Knights Errernt' (1675), British Museum, Sloane MS. 360, cited in F.H.A. Aalen, 'The evolution of the traditional house' p.56. 17 E. Wakefield, *An account of Ireland statistical and political* (2 vols, London, 1812), ii, p. 751. 18 Arthur Young drew an important sketch of the poor housing he observed in Ireland in the 1770s. It is re-produced in F.H.A. Aalen, K. Whelan & M. Stout (eds), *Atlas of the Irish rural landscape* (Cork, 1997), p.75. 19 Ibid., p. 44. 20 These townlands are still referred to as 'Llyod's land'. 21 Jones to King, 28 March 1817. Most of the correspondence between Lloyd and King has been published as F.S.L. Lyons, 'Vicissitudes of a middleman in County Leitrim 1810–27' *Irish Historical Studies*, 9:35 (March 1955), pp 300–19. 22 *First report from select committee on the state of disease and conditions of the labouring poor in Ireland*, HC 1819, vii, p. 314. 23 Llyod to King, 10 August 1822, in Lyons, 'vicissitudes', p. 316. 24 H. Heaney (ed.), *A Scottish Whig in Ireland, 1835–38: the Irish journals of Robert Graham of Redgorton* (Dublin, 1999), p. 286. 25 Supplement to Appendix E, (see note 1 above), p.15. Eight years earlier the Revd John Maguire wrote to the Catholic Association pleading that the 'people of this poor parish [Kiltubrid] ... being at present destitute of money' were unable to pay the Catholic rent. See *Roscommon Journal*, 4 Oct. 1828. 26 Supplement to Appendix E, (see note 1), p. 17. 27 Ibid. 28 *Evidence taken before the commissioners appointed to inquire into the occupation of land in Ireland*, Devon Report, HC, 1845, xx, p. 245. 29 Captain Edward Wynne was an inspector for the Board of Works in Clare and later was a Poor Law Inspector for Leitrim and Roscommon. Controversy followed him wherever he went. See D. Fitzpatrick, 'Famine, entitlements and seduction: Captain Edmond Wynne in Ireland, 1846–51', *English Historical Review*, 110, (1995), pp 596–619; L. Kennedy, 'Bastardy and the Great Famine' in Carla King (ed.), *Famine, land and culture in Ireland* (Dublin, 2000), p. 9; Cormac Ó Gráda, *Black '47 and beyond, The Great Irish Famine in history, economy and memory* (Princeton, 2000), pp 53, 59–66, and 247–8; D. Thomson, *Woodbrook* (London, 1974), pp 156–72. 30 *Report from the select committee of the House of Lords appointed to investigate and report upon all the allegations and charges contained in the petition to the Board of Guardians of the Union of Carrick on Shannon complaining of the management and misconduct of the late*

Vice Guardians of the said Union (Appendix B), HL 1850, xxii, p.332.   **31** Ibid., p. 333.   **32** Census of Ireland 1841 and 1851. **33** There were 20 houses in Corderry Peyton in 1856. Sixteen of these had holdings of five acres or under. See *Griffith's Valuation*.   **34** The population of this townland dropped from 46 in 1841 to just one in 1851.   **35** *Supplement to Appendix F, First report of commissioners for inquiring into the condition of the poorer classes in Ireland*, HC, 1836, xxxiii, p. 15.   **36** See P. Flanagan, *The Ballinamore & Ballyconnell Canal*.   **37** Census of Ireland 1841. All the other Connacht counties had a higher percentage of one-roomed houses at this time. See A. Gailey, 'The housing of the rural poor in nineteenth-century Ulster' in *Ulster Folklife*, 22 (1976), p. 37.   **38** The decline in the number of one-roomed houses between 1841 and 1851 was even greater in Co. Monaghan than in Leitrim. See P. Duffy, 'The Famine in County Monaghan' in C. Kinealy & T. Parkhill (eds), *The Famine in Ulster* (Belfast, 1997), p. 189. The one-roomed houses survived longer along the west coast of Ireland. **39** Census of Ireland 1841.   **40** NAI, Census of Ireland 1901.   **41** For a comparison between the percentage of one-roomed houses in Leitrim and in other counties see Gailey, as per note 37 above.   **42** *Evidence taken before the commissioners appointed to inquire into the occupation of land in Ireland*, Devon Report, HC, 1845, xx, p. 245.   **43** See Rossy National School roll book for 1879 where some of his children were attending school. In it he is described as a 'drover'. See also the NAI, Census of Ireland 1901.   **44** NAI, Census of Ireland 1901.   **45** They had seven children born between 1868 and 1886. See Roman Catholic baptismal register for the parish of Kiltubrid.   **46** See civil register of deaths for Co. Leitrim. Kate Bearer was 65 years old.   **47** This house still stands, though in a ruinous state. It was surveyed by Liam Kelly on 14 April 2003. **48** Gailey, (see note 37 above), pp 39–40.   **49** K. Danaher, *Ireland's vernacular architecture* (Dublin, 1975), p. 39; see also photograph WAG 1196 in the Ulster Folk and Transport Museum.   **50** For a description of the development of these houses see S. Moore, 'The development of working class housing in Ireland 1840–1912: a study of housing conditions, built form and policy' (PhD thesis, University of Ulster, Coleraine, 1986), pp 1–85.   **51** NAI, Census of Ireland 1901.   **52** Ibid. **53** Ibid.   **54** Department of Irish Folklore, UCD, no. 5680, MS. 5210, p. 300. This description would suggest that it was a mud-walled house.   **55** The photograph of Whelan's house in the townland of Driney, which Duncan took on 21 August 1892, shows the full door open and the half door closed. Kelly, *The face of time*, p. 56. All his other photographs of cottages show them with both doors closed. See also Gailey, *Rural houses of the north of Ireland* (Edinburgh, 1984), pp 133–4. **56** Whitewash was used to help prevent the spread of typhus. See Gailey, *Rural houses of the north of Ireland*, pp 63–5. Virtually all of the houses photographed in the Kiltubrid area by Duncan were whitewashed.   **57** Gailey, *Rural houses of the north of Ireland*, pp 107–8; A. Day & P. McWilliams (eds), *Ordnance Survey memoirs of Ireland, parishes of Fermanagh*, (Belfast, 1995), pp 11–12.   **58** NAI, Census of Ireland 1901.   **59** Henry Doran's report is based on all of the parish of Kiltubrid and a small mountainous area of Ballinaglera parish to the north of it. See J. Morrissey (ed.), *On the verge of want* (Dublin, 2001), p. 67. **60** Morrisey (ed.), *On the verge of want*, p. 71.   **61** Ibid. p. 67.   **62** Duncan arranged all his 1889 photographs neatly into an album. He titled the album 'A holiday in Ireland, views at and near Annadale, Carrick-on-Shannon, Co. Leitrim, August 1889' and he gave each photograph a caption. This detailed and meticulous approach renders the photographs more valuable as a primary source for the study of the period. He took two photographs of this mud cabin, but for some reason, perhaps to avoid embarrassment, he did not name the occupants. The house was situated in the Rossy/Castlefore area. See Kelly, *The face of time*, pp 32 & 33.   **63** E.E. Evans, 'Sod and turf houses in Ireland' in J.G. Jenkins (ed.), *Studies in folk life* (London, 1969), pp 80–90.   **64** C. Ó Danachair, 'Materials and methods in Irish traditional building' in *Journal of the Royal Society of Antiquaries of Ireland*, 87 (1957), p. 63.   **65** See Kelly, *The face of time*, p. 33.   **66** Census of Ireland 1901.   **67** Ibid.   **68** S. Lewis, *Topographical dictionary of Ireland* (2 vols, Dublin, 1837), ii, p.217.   **69** Morrissey (ed.), *On the verge of want*, p.75.   **70** See Duncan's photograph of Driney House in Kelly, *The face of time*, p.38. Aughacashel House still stands and is used as a dwelling house.   **71** Kelly, *The face of time*, p. 31.   **72** The parish priest of Kiltubrid, Henry Kennedy, lived in Letterfine House from 1855 until his death in 1876.   **73** Kelly, *The face of time*, p.18. Laheen House can be usefully compared with Berwick Hall, in Co. Down. See H. Dixon, *An introduction to Ulster architecture* (Belfast, 1975), p. 31; B. Ní Fhloinn & G. Dennison (eds), *Traditional architecture in Ireland* (Dublin, 1994), p.61; K. Danaher, *Ireland's vernacular architecture* (Dublin, 1975), pp 40–1. **74** John Peyton married Catherine Reynolds of Loughscur c.1650 and it seems likely that they built Laheen House. See Sir B. Burke, *Landed gentry of Ireland*, (London, 1912), pp 562–3.   **75** Aalen, 'The evolution of the traditional house in western Ireland', pp 47–58.   **76** Lewis, *Topographical dictionary of Ireland*, ii, p. 217.   **77** Kelly, *The face of time*, p. 50; NAI, Census of Ireland 1901.   **78** NAI, Census of Ireland 1901. The curate, John O'Farrell, lived in a five-roomed house.   **79** The servants' quarters were at the back. This is not shown in the photograph.   **80** My thanks to Steve Barrett, a descendant of the family pictured in front of Laheen House, for giving me a copy of this photograph.   **81** Moore, 'The development of working class housing in Ireland', p.109.

2. LAND

1 M.J. Winstanley, *Ireland and the land question, 1800–1922* (London & New York, 1984), pp 8–9; B.L. Solow, *The land question and the Irish economy, 1870–1903* (Harvard, 1971), pp 98–101.   **2** Solow, *The land question and the Irish economy, 1870–1903*, p. 111.   **3** *Leitrim Advertiser*, 30 Sept. 1880.   **4** The unpublished diary of Leland L. Duncan is part of the private papers of the Slacke family.   **5** Unpublished diary of Duncan, p. 3.   **6** *First report of commissioners for inquiring into the condition of the poorer lasses in Ireland* (Appendix F), HC, 1836, xxxiii, p. 361.   **7** Ibid. p. 88.   **9** *Agricultural statistics for the year 1891, observations on the produce of the crops*, HC, 1892, lxxxviii, p.89.   **10** Wakefield, *An account of Ireland*, ii, p.751.   **11** Ibid. **12** McParlan, *Statistical survey of County Leitrim*, p. 29.   **13** Ploughs were especially scarce in Leitrim. McParlan stated that the people there prefer 'this machine [the loy] to ploughs.'   **14** *First report of commissioners for inquiring into the condition of the poorer classes in Ireland*, (Appendix F), HC, 1836, xxxiii, p 361.   **15** Ibid., p.363. People working as pack animals was common in Leitrim, especially in the pre-Famine decades. Robert Jones, writing about the neighbouring parish of Fenagh in 1815, stated that 'themselves [tenant farmers], their wives and children were drawing clay and sand *on their backs* in little baskets and reclaiming the boggs and verges in hopes of making a bit of meadow'. Cited in Lyons, 'Select documents, pp 310–11. Things had not changed much 21 years later when it was reported that the labourers in Leitrim could be 'seen drawing in baskets on their backs, the gravel and lime' in order to reclaim bog land. See *First report of commissioners for inquiring into the condition of the* *poorer classes in Ireland* (Appendix E), HC, 1836, xxxii, p. 39. **16** Morrissey (ed.), *On the verge of want*, p. 68. **17** See Kelly, *The face of time*, p. 65. **18** Ibid., p.40. **19** Evans, *Irish folkways* (London,1989 edition), p.190. **20** Ibid., pp 128, 136 & 190. **21** Fr Dan Gallogly, *Sliabh an Iarainn Slopes* (Cavan, 1991), p. 290. **22** Many of his photographs have been published in B.M.Walker, *Sentry Hill: an Ulster farm and family* (Belfast, 1981). **23** Walker, *Sentry Hill*, pp 89, 91, 94 & 102–3. **24** McParlan, *Statistical survey of County Leitrim*, p.25. **25** Wakefield, *An account of Ireland*, ii, p.751. **26** Ibid., p. 752. **27** P. Gaskell, *Morvern transformed: a highland parish in the nineteenth century* (Cambridge, 1980), Appendix A, p. 121. **28** *Report of commissioners for inquiring into the condition of the poorer classes in Ireland*, Appendix F., HC, 1836, xxxiii, p.363. **29** Morrissey (ed.), *On the verge of want*, p. 71. **30** Ibid., p.70. **31** Unpublished 1892 pocket diary of Leland L. Duncan, p. 5. **32** One of these photographs has been published in Kelly, *The face of time*, p.66. **33** Ibid. p. 36. In 1809 it was said that 'when a man is seen riding in this part of Ireland on a pie-bald horse, it is considered as a sign of his being a doctor.' See Wakefield, *An account of Ireland*, ii, p. 752. **34** Kelly, *The face of time*, p. 67. **35** Ibid. p. 42. **36** The number of stables in the parish would suggest that only one out of every eight households had a horse. This is quite low, even for the west of Ireland. For example in Grange, Co. Sligo, which was also designated a congested district, one out of every four households had a horse. See Morrissey (ed.), *On the verge of want*, p. 57. **37** *Agricultural statistics for the year 1890*, HC, 1890–91, xci, p.78. **38** Morrissey (ed.), *On the verge of want*, p.68 **39** McParlan, *Statistical survey of County Leitrim*, p. 10. **40** Ibid., pp 49–56. **41** *Evidence taken before the commissioners appointed to inquire into the occupation of land in Ireland*, HC, 1845, xx, p. 245. **42** Morrissey (ed.), *On the verge of want*, p. 71. **43** Ibid., p. 73. **44** McParlan, *Statistical survey of County Leitrim*, pp 27–8; *Appendix F to first report of commissioners for inquiring into the condition of the poorer classes in Ireland*, HC, 1836, xxxiii, p. 362. **45** *Evidence taken before the commissioners*, HC, 1845, xx, p. 246. **46** Ibid., p. 269. **47** Ibid., p. 277. **48** *First report of commissioners for inquiring into the condition of the poorer classes in Ireland*, Appendix F., 1836, xxxviii, p.361. **49** *Evidence taken before the commissioners*, HC, 1845, xx, p.271. **50** Morrissey (ed.) *On the verge of want*, p. 68. **51** Ibid. **52** *Leitrim Advertiser*, 23 Oct. 1879. **53** An t-Athair Domhnall Mac an Ghalloglaigh, 'The Land League in Leitrim, 1879–1883' in *Breifne*, 6:22 (1983–4), pp 156–7. **54** Ibid., pp 169–70. The killing of Philip Meehan, a great granduncle of mine, was seen by Michael Davitt as an event of some significance in the land struggle. See M. Davitt, *Fall of feudalism* (London & New York, 1904), p. 263. **55** Mac an Ghalloglaigh, 'The Land League in Leitrim' p. 168. **56** *Leitrim Advertiser*, 30 Sept. 1880. **57** Ibid. **58** *Leitrim Advertiser*, 2 July 1881. **59** Private papers of the Slacke family. **60** See Liam Kelly, *A flame now quenched: rebels and Frenchmen in Leitrim, 1793–98* (Dublin, 1998), pp 19–66. **61** McParlan, *Statistical survey of County Leitrim*, pp 43–4. **62** Ibid., p. 44. **63** *First report of commissioners for inquiring into the condition of the poorer classes in Ireland* (Appendix F), HC, 1836, xxxiii, p. 213. **64** C. Ó Danachair, 'Farmyard forms and their distribution in Ireland' in *Ulster Folklife*, 27 (1981), pp 63–76; D. McCourt, 'The house with bedroom over byre: a long-house derivative?' in *Ulster Folklife*, 15 (1970), pp 3–19. **65** See Duncan's photographs of outhouses in Kelly, *The face of time*, pp 35, 41, 43 & 52. **66** Morrissey (ed.), *On the verge of want*, p.71. **67** Ibid., p.70. **68** Ibid., p.71. Normally the coolest room, the one farthest away from the fire, was used as a dairy. **69** Ibid., pp 68–9. **70** For example, in the Lough Eask district of Donegal it was reported that 'sheep are a good deal kept.' Morrissey, *On the verge of want*, p. 32. **71** Ibid., p. 68. **72** In 1836 the Revd Charles Clarke complained of 'the great want of barns and proper threshing floors' in the barony of Mohill. He went on to say that 'in moist seasons the oats are threshed on the uneven, and in many cases, moist floor of the cabin; in clearer weather on the harder surface of the road.' See *First report of commissioners for inquiring into the condition of the poorer classes in Ireland*, (Appendix F), HC, 1836, xxxiii, p. 363. **73** Walker, *Sentry Hill*, p.86. The hay-sheds photographed by William McKinney are large three or four bay sheds. They were constructed with steel and corrugated iron and were finished off with eave runs and down-pipes. The size and the quality of these sheds emphasize the gulf between farming in Co. Antrim and in Co. Leitrim where the out-houses were small stone structures covered in thatch. **74** Morrissey (ed.), *On the verge of want*, p. 70. **75** See photographs of rick building by Duncan in Kelly, *The face of time*, pp 64 & 65. **76** Ibid., p. 41. **77** Morrissey (ed.), *On the verge of want*, p. 68. **78** Straw nests were hung for the hens on the cow-byre walls. For the type of straw nests in Leitrim see Evans, *Irish folkways*, p. 61.

3. PEOPLE

1 Cited in Morrissey (ed.), *On the verge of want*, p. vii. **2** W.L. Micks, *An account of the constitution, administration and dissolution of the Congested Districts Board for Ireland from 1891 to 1923* (Dublin, 1925), p. 7. **3** Lewis, *Topographical dictionary of Ireland*, ii, p. 217. **4** Census of Ireland 1841. **5** Register of Kiltubrid Roman Catholic Church. It was not unusual to have multiple pre-Lenten weddings at this time. **6** The percentage drop in the number of houses in the parish in this period was 21.4 per cent. See fig. 2.3. The drop in population in Kiltubrid was slightly less than the 27.94 per cent drop for Co. Leitrim as a whole. Leitrim had the fifth highest percentage drop in population in Ireland between 1841 and 1851. The neighbouring counties of Roscommon, Sligo and Cavan were higher; so too was Mayo. See W.E. Vaughan & A.J. Fitzpatrick (eds), *Irish historical statistics, population 1821–1971* (Dublin, 1978), pp 5–16. **7** See figure 1.2. **8** Census of Ireland 1841 and 1851. **9** See fig. 3.1. **10** *Leitrim Advertiser*, 28 August 1879, 18 September 1879 and 23 October 1879. **11** *Reports and tables relating to migratory agricultural Irish labourers for 1880*, HC, 1881, xciii, p. 807. **12** See fig. 3.2; S.H. Cousens, 'Emigration and demographic change in Ireland, 1851–1861' in *Economic History Review*, 14:2 (1961), pp 275–6; Vaughan & Fitzpatrick (eds), *Irish historical statistics*, p. 334. **13** *First report of commissioners for inquiring into the condition of the poorer classes in Ireland*, Appendix F, HC, 1836, xxxiii, p. 15. **14** See the Catholic Church records for Kiltubrid. These marriage records indicate that New York, Boston, Worcester and Providence in the United States and Liverpool, Glasgow and Edinburgh in Great Britain were the destinations Kiltubrid people were most likely to emigrate to. **15** Morrissey (ed.), *On the verge of want*, p. 69. **16** B.M. Kerr, 'Irish seasonal migration to Great Britain, 1800–38' in *Irish Historical Studies*, 3:12 (1943), pp 365–79; D.M. MacRaild, *Irish migrants in modern Britain, 1750–1922* (London, 1999), pp 44–5. **17** See J. Boyle, 'A marginal figure: the Irish rural labourer' in S. Clarke & J.S. Donnelly (eds), *Irish peasants, violence and political unrest, 1780–1914*, (Dublin, 1983), pp 320–1. **18** *Reports and tables relating to migratory agricultural Irish labourers for 1882*, HC, (1882), lxxiv, p.169. **19** *Agricultural statistics, Ireland 1891, reports and tables relating to migratory agricultural labourers*, HC, (1891), xci, p. 526. **20** Morrissey (ed.), *On the verge of want*, p. 69. **21** District Inspector's observation book for Keshcarrigan National School, p. 5. **22** Morrissey (ed.), *On the verge* *of want*, p. 72. **23** Leland L.Duncan, 'Folk-lore gleanings from County Leitrim' in *Folk-lore*, 4:2 (June 1893), p. 176. **24** *Roscommon Herald*, 27 April 1889. For an account of the setting up of the Gaelic Athletic Association in Kiltubrid see Liam Kelly, *Kiltubrid* (1984), pp 26–54. Francis Kellegher from Kilclare was the first secretary of the 'Kiltubrid Michael Davitt' club. His reports on the club's activities were regularly printed in the pro nationalist *Roscommon Herald* newspaper. **25** *Leitrim Advertiser*, 6 June 1889. **26** *Roscommon Herald*, 18 May 1889. **27** Ibid., 9 Nov. 1889. **28** Ibid., 16 Nov. 1889. **29** Ibid., 16 Feb. 1891. **30** Ibid., 23 March 1891. **31** *Leitrim Advertiser*, 9 May 1891. **32** Kelly, *Kiltubrid*, pp 52–4. Fr Quinn was curate in Kiltubrid from 1890 to 1894. See the *Irish Catholic Directory* for the years 1890 to 1894. **33** *Roscommon Herald*, 20 Feb. 1892. **34** Kelly, *Kiltubrid*, pp 56–63. **35** The fact that Aghacashlaun set up a GAA club in 1918 and Kilclare in 1928 would suggest that there was more than one community in the section of the parish we have marked 'B' in figure 4.3. See Kelly, *Kiltubrid*, pp 64–79. **36** *Leitrim Observer*, 20 November 1909. **37** It was built as a barn church in 1781 and was converted into a much larger cruciform church in 1891. **38** J. Morrissey (ed.), *On the verge of want*, pp 72 and 76. **39** Flanagan, *The Cavan & Leitrim railway*. Leland Duncan travelled from Annadale to Ballinamore on 13 August 1892. The single fare cost 7d. See his unpublished 1892 pocket diary. **40** Cited in B. Griffin, 'The early history of cycling in Meath and Drogheda' in *Riocht na Midhe*, 15 (2000), p. 143. **41** Ibid. **42** Interview with Thomas Kelly of Laheen, Keshcarrigan, Co. Leitrim (12 June 2004). **43** Bridget was born in 1862. John (1865) died in infancy. Another brother also called John, was born in 1869, Hugh (1871), Catherine (1873) and Eliza (1877). **44** M. McManus, 'Folk-lore gleanings from County Leitrim' in *Folk-Lore* 4:2 (June 1893), pp 176–94. Duncan wrote in his introduction: 'These tales were related to me by a little lad of fourteen whose mother, in her turn, heard them in her youth from her father, John Tighe of Corderry Peyton, the son of Peter Tighe of Corrick beside Laheen Peyton (Co. Leitrim), both of whom were Irish speakers and spoken of as great storytellers.' **45** See Duncan's unpublished 1892 diary. **46** Ibid. **47** Kelly, *The face of time*, p. 62. **48** For information on the Slacke family see H.A. Crofton, *Records of the Slacke family in Ireland* (not dated but about appears to be a late 19th century publication); Kelly, *The face of time*; The private papers of the Slacke family. **49** See L. Kelly, 'The growth of Methodism in Cavan & Leitrim 1750–1800' in *Breifne*, 10:38 (2002), pp 454–95. **50** Census of Ireland 1891. **51** *Leitrim Observer*, 2 April 1904 and 14 April 1904. **52** *Leitrim Advertiser*, 13 October, 1901. **53** Ibid., 30 January 1908. **54** Kelly, *The face of time*, pp 25–6. **55** Laura Jones does an important critique of W.A. Green's somewhat similar photograph taken in Inishowen. She concludes that 'photographic evidence tends to be corroborative rather than definitive ... [photographs] are a very useful addition to the range of devices through which an attempt may be made to build up a picture of life in the past.' See L. Jones, 'Photography and ethnological research' in *Ulster Folklife*, 26 (1980), pp 65–8. See also *Ulster Folklife*, 19 (1973), pp 24–9 and *Ulster Folklife*, 21 (1975), pp 10–14. **56** This woman bears a remarkable resemblance, in both expression and dress, to Mrs Margaret McGaw who was photographed by William Fee McKinney in Co. Antrim in 1870. See Walker, *Sentry Hill*, p. 32. **57** The Ward's were relatively well off. They had 18.5 acres of land which was valued at £7. See Griffith's *Valuation of tenements, parish of Kiltubrid*, p.108. **58** It would appear that very little spinning or weaving was carried on in Kiltubrid at this time. Henry Doran's detailed report to the Congested Districts Board, two years after this photograph was taken, stated that only 'a very small number of people who have sheep on the mountain make flannels, socks, stockings, and a small quantity of frieze for their own use, but not for sale.' Morrissey (ed.) *On the verge of want*, p. 69. **59** Kelly, *The face of time*, pp 55 and 56. **60** Griffith's Valuation. **61** Census of Ireland 1901. **62** Ibid. **63** Duncan's unpublished 1892 pocket diary. **64** Ibid. **65** Kelly, *The face of time*, p.40. **66** See front cover. **67** My thanks to bernie Meehan, Moheravogagh, Co. Leitrim, for giving me this information in a letter recieved on 15 February 1996. **68** Kelly, *The face of time*, p.65. **69** Eleven of the others in the meitheal wore caps rather than hats. Four, including Mikey Lynch, wore hats and one young man had no headgear at all. **70** See Kelly, *The face of time*, pp 39, 40 and 65. **71** L. Duncan, 'Fairy beliefs and other folklore notes from County Leitrim' in *Folklore* 7:2, no.2 (June, 1896), pp 170–1. **72** They lived in Driney. See Kelly, *The face of time*, pp 56 and 57; **73** She was a servant at Annadale House. **74** He was a native of Cootehill in Co. Cavan and worked at Annadale House as a coachman. **75** For other folklore gathered in Kiltubrid by Leland L. Duncan see 'Folk-lore gleanings from County Leitrim' in *Folk-lore*, 4:2 (June 1893), pp 176–94; 'Further notes from County Leitrim,' *Folk-lore*, 5:3 (Sept. 1894), pp 177–216; 'Irish folktales' in *Folk-lore*, 6:3, (Sept. 1895), pp 308–10; 'Fairy beliefs and other folk-lore from County Leitrim', in *Folk-lore*, vii, 7:20 (June 1896), pp 161–83; 'The quicken tree of Dubhros' in *Folk-lore*, 7:2 (December 1896), pp 321–30. **76** A. Bourke, *The burning of Bridget Cleary* (London, 1999). **77** M.J.F. McCarthy, *Five years in Ireland, 1895–1999* (Dublin, 1901), pp 66–9. **78** McParlan, *Statistical survey of the county of Leitrim*, p. 63. **79** General Jean Sarrazin, *Notes sur l'Expedition d'Irlande*, translated as 'An officer's account of the French Campaign in Ireland in 1798' in *Irish Sword*, 2 (1954–6), p. 111. See also Kelly, *A flame now quenched*, p. 77. **80** Wakefield, *An account of Ireland*, ii, p. 751. **81** *First report of commissioners for inquiring into the condition of the poorer classes in Ireland*, Appendix E., HC, (1836), xxxiii, p. 69. **82** Ibid., p.70. **83** Ibid., p.69. **84** Ibid., p. 69. **85** Morrissey (ed.), *On the verge of want*, p. 71. **86** Jones, 'Photography and ethnological research', pp 65–8. **87** Ibid., p.65. **88** Kelly, *The face of time*, pp 32, 33 and 60. **89** See Duncan's photograph album titled 'A holiday in Ireland, views at and near Annadale, Carrick-on-Shannon, Co. Leitrim in August 1889.' 'Fair' is used here in the sense of being beautiful rather than light coloured. **90** Kelly, *The face of time*, pp 55 and 56. **91** Ibid., p.6. **92** Griffith's Valuation. **93** Ellen Ward was baptised on 8 March 1868. See Kiltubrid Roman Catholic parish records. She started in Rossy National School on 18 September 1874 and left it on 11 November 1882. See Register of Rossy National School, p. 31. **94** Kelly, *The face of time*, p.56. **95** Adelia M. West, unpublished memoirs, p. 42. **96** Ibid., p. 43. **97** N.A.I., R.P. 620/22/19; Kelly, *A flame now quenched*, p. 32. **98** *Evidence taken before the commissioners appointed to inquire into the occupation of land in Ireland*, HC, 1845, xx, p.270. **99** Ibid. p. 277. **100** Morrissey (ed.), *On the verge of want*, p. 71. **101** Ibid.

CONCLUSION

1 Morrissey (ed.), *On the verge of want*, p. 70. **2** I found the Duncan photographs relating to Leitrim in private hands in west Cork. My thanks to Florence Easterbrook-Reynolds and Sandra Vernon for putting me on the right trail.